2614

COMPENSATORY EDUCATION

FOR CULTURAL DEPRIVATION

BENJAMIN S. BLOOM
ALLISON DAVIS
ROBERT HESS
Department of Education
University of Chicago

LC
4065
.B55

Based on working papers contributed by participants
in the

RESEARCH CONFERENCE ON
EDUCATION AND CULTURAL DEPRIVATION

151226

HOLT, RINEHART AND WINSTON, INC.
New York   Chicago   San Francisco   Toronto   London

RESEARCH CONFERENCE

ON

EDUCATION AND CULTURAL DEPRIVATION

June 8 - 12, University of Chicago

Participants

Anastasi, Anne(Dept. of Psychology, Fordham Univ.)
Bernstein, Basil (Dept. of Sociology, Univ. of London)
Bloom, Benjamin (Dept. of Education, Univ. of Chicago)
Bloom, Sophie (Howland School, Chicago)
Chase, Francis (Dept. of Education, Univ. of Chicago)
Davis, Allison (Dept. of Education, Univ. of Chicago)
Deutsch, Martin (Institute for Developmental Studies,
          New York Medical College)
Douglass, Joseph (Chief, Program Analysis and Scientific
          Communications Staff, NIMH)
Erikson, Erik (Dept. of Psychology, Harvard Univ.)
Fowler, William (Dept. of Education, Univ. of Chicago)
Gallagher, James (Institute for Research on Exceptional
          Children, Univ. of Illinois)
Getzels, Jacob (Dept. of Education, Univ. of Chicago)
Gordon, Edmund (Dept. of Educational Psychology and
          Guidance, Yeshiva Univ.)
Gottlieb, David (School of Education, Michigan State Univ.)
Gray, Susan (Dept. of Psychology, George Peabody College)
Havighurst, Robert (Depts. of Human Development and Edu-
          cation, Univ. of Chicago)
Hess, Robert (Depts. of Human Development and Education,
          Univ. of Chicago)
Iscoe, Ira (Dept. of Psychology, Univ. of Texas)
Jensen, Arthur (School of Education, Univ. of California)
Kohlberg, Lawrence (Depts. of Psychology and Human De-
          velopment, Univ. of Chicago)
Kravitz, Ida (Reading Supervisor - School District of
          Philadelphia)
Lane, Hugh (Dept. of Education, Univ. of Chicago)
Lewis, Hylan (Dept. of Sociology, Howard Univ.)
Lighthall, Frederick F. (Dept. of Education, Univ. of
          Chicago)
Lortie, Dan (Dept. of Education, Univ. of Chicago)
Marburger, Carl (Great Cities Schools Improvement Pro-
          gram - Detroit)

Pettigrew, Thomas (Dept. of Social Relations, Harvard
          Univ.)
Robinson, Helen (Dept. of Education, Univ. of Chicago)
Silverman, Susan (Research Asst., Dept. of Education,
          Univ. of Chicago)
Smilansky, Moshe (Henrietta Szold Institute for Child
          and Youth Welfare - Israel)
Stanley, Julian (Laboratory of Experimental Design,
          Univ. of Wisconsin)

Observers

DeVinney, Leland (Rockefeller Foundation)
Goslin, David (Russell Sage Foundation)
Saltzman, Henry (Ford Foundation)
Seeley, David (U. S. Office of Education)
Singer, Arthur (Carnegie Foundation)

Foreword

The Research Conference on Education and Cultural Deprivation was held at the University of Chicago, June 8-12, 1964, to review what is already known about the problems of education and cultural deprivation, to make recommendations about what might be done to solve some of these problems, and to suggest the critical problems for further research.

Working in small groups as well as in meetings of the whole, the participants in the conference attempted to formulate and document a series of generalizations about education and cultural deprivation. These generalizations draw on what is known from a body of theory and principles, what is known from relevant empirical research, and what is known from observations and action programs in the school. Although as scholars and research workers we differ in our criteria of certainty, we have attempted to formulate our statements on what is known sufficiently clearly to warrant action, policy formulation, or a new way of viewing a problem or task. This is a far cry from knowledge that is certain and definitive.

The group then proceeded to indicate some of the implications of this knowledge for the work of the schools. It is this material that is the basis for this report. While all members of the group contributed to the basic materials, responsibility for the final report must rest with the Committee (Bloom, Davis, and Hess) which planned the conference and which subsequently wrote the first draft of this report. This report has been revised on the basis of suggestions and criticisms submitted by individual members of the conference. Still, it is recognized that the final responsibility for this report must be placed on the committee rather than the group as a whole.

We wish to express our gratitude to the U. S. Office of Education for encouragement and support for the Research Conference.

Acknowledgments

There are many persons who participated in the preparation of the basic documents and materials on which this report is based. The participants in the Conference are listed on page II. Each of them gave approximately a week to the seminars and discussions which produced the working papers on which this report is based. They also read and criticized the drafts of the reports and helped greatly in the preparation of the final statement.

Miss Susan Silverman served as the Research Assistant who took charge of many aspects of this conference including the preparation of the annotated bibliography. She also helped greatly in the revision of the report.

Mrs. Linda Hutts and Mrs. Estell Jones served as secretaries for the conference and took responsibility for putting the materials including the report and the bibliography in a readable form. Mrs. Jones did much to relieve the committee of many of the details of running the conference, getting the report reproduced, and finally in preparing the report for publication.

Miss Silverman was helped in preparing the annotated bibliography by William Hall, Forest Harrison, Barbara Lee, Linn Orear, and Phyllis Vosbeck.

We were helped in the editing of these manuscripts by David Bloom and Mrs. Constantino.

Funds for this work were provided by the Cooperative Research Program of the U. S. Office of Education, U. S. Department of Health, Education and Welfare, under Contract HEW-OE-4-10-256.

Benjamin S. Bloom
Allison Davis
Robert Hess

Preface

Very few problems in the field of education are as complex as the problems of cultural deprivation. An adequate attack on these educational problems requires that educational policy makers, curriculum specialists, teachers, guidance workers, and administrators have an appreciation of the many ways in which the social problems of our society bear directly on the development of the child and adolescent and influence the interaction between students and the schools.

We find very few individuals who have a thorough grasp of how the many disciplines of the behavioral sciences are involved in understanding or attacking these problems. In order to secure a more comprehensive picture of the problems of education and cultural deprivation we found it necessary to bring together leading specialists from many different disciplines. With the aid of background papers and an extensive annotated bibliography, we were able to get working groups in the Research Conference on Education and Cultural Deprivation to analyze the problems with due recognition of the many facets of these problems.

In Part I of this volume, we have attempted to summarize what we regard as known about the nature of cultural deprivation, especially as it relates to the educational process. This summarization is made as clearly and as simply as we could find the words to express it. We have tried to inform the readers of this report as to the bases on which we made this analysis by a series of appendix notes, by the references we have cited, and by the use of a detailed annotated bibliography of some of the works which bear most directly on these problems. This bibliography constitutes Part II of this volume.

It is our hope that this material will be used by groups of teachers, other educational specialists, and community groups in order to inform themselves about what is already known about education and cultural deprivation. It is to be hoped that these materials will be used in seminars and discussions by teachers in every school which has some children who suffer from cultural deprivation. In order to simplify this process, we have organized our report so as to approximate the different levels of education in the schools as they are now organized. While there may be some room for interpretation of this knowledge, we do not expect that the careful reader will find himself in serious disagreement with this aspect of our work.

We have then gone on to make clear what we believe the implications of this knowledge to be for the schools, the communities, and the nation. Here we attempt to make clear a set of value positions as to where responsibility rests for the solution of these problems. We have tried to be as explicit as possible about these value positions. They express the views of a careful and objective group of social scientists about what is realistically possible in our society. Here, we do expect that there will be disagreement in schools and communities about the placement of responsibility for attacking these problems. There are differences in emphasis in social philosophy about the home, the school, and the community and we hope that such differences will be made as explicit as possible and then examined in the light of alternative views of these issues. However, we would urge that school and community groups use this report as a basis for recognizing when they differ on the relevant knowledge and information and when they differ on the value issues and the placement of responsibility.

Finally, we have made a series of recommendations for dealing with these problems insofar as they affect the schools and education. Here is where we expect that school and community groups will differ most sharply from us and from each other. It is our hope that such groups will study these recommendations very carefully and will read the supporting appendix notes and references before discarding or accepting these recommendations. There must be a variety of alternative solutions to these problems. We would urge that groups which take exception to our recommendations propose alternatives which are as carefully conceived as we have tried to make ours. To do nothing is really not an alternative to the recommendations we have made in this report.

Thus, we hope that this report and the supporting documentation will enable school personnel, community groups, and state and national bodies and organizations to study and eventually to solve a series of educational and social problems which are very far reaching in their scope--the problems of education and cultural deprivation.

CONTENTS

Part 1

A Report on

COMPENSATORY EDUCATION FOR CULTURAL DEPRIVATION

Introduction

Section 1

Throughout the world, school systems have developed elementary- and secondary-school curricula and programs which appear to work relatively well for a sizeable proportion of the students. Perhaps as many as one-half of the entering students are able to complete these programs successfully, if financial and other obstacles do not loom too large. These educational programs are increasingly the determiners of status and economic opportunity, and completion of a secondary-school program is rapidly becoming the minimal requirement for successful entry into the larger society. Especially in the highly developed nations, the individual who is not able to complete secondary school is denied admission to an ever increasing sector of the occupational system.[1]

As long as there was ample opportunity in the economy for unskilled workers with a minimum of education, the thought and energy of educators could be directed to the continual weeding out of the scholastically less able and the selection of the more able to get more and more education and specialization. The lives and careers adversely affected by this selection process have not been a central concern of school people. So much thought and effort was directed to the final products of the educational system--the graduates of the system--that the underlying assumptions and methods of the system were rarely questioned.

Now we are in the midst of such basic social changes that it is appropriate to use the term "revolution." These social changes are affecting the entire fabric of our society and will increasingly affect all aspects of the educational system. What are some of the social changes which are so far-reaching?[2]

First, a rapidly developing, complex, urban, industrial society which requires that functioning members of this society be highly literate, responsive to rapid changes in every area of life and work, and able to learn and re-learn complex ideas and skills as minimal conditions for economic security, social maturity, and independence.

1

Second, rising levels of aspirations of individuals and groups that have been long submerged or placed in marginal positions. These aspirations are for a larger share in the affluence of the society and for the education which will make this possible. Underlying this is the insistence on personal dignity and freedom and a search for a new sense of identity.

Third, increasing responsiveness of government to the needs and pressures of individuals as well as subgroups in the population. Social ills that might have gone unchecked for many decades previously can now be made central in the concerns of government and the courts.

Fourth, a rising level of affluence which makes further material goals for many individuals somewhat subordinate to other goals such as security and interpersonal relations. There is an increasing quest for personal identity and a set of values which will make life more meaningful.

These forces and changes in the society and culture will not permit any social institution to meet the new conditions and needs without modification, whether the institution be government, business and industry, religion, welfare, or education. It is these forces which require a major reshaping of our educational institutions.

It is difficult at present to determine the exact way in which educational institutions in the United States will be reshaped over the next decade. It is likely that one major change will be a shift in the conception of education from a status-giving and selective system to a system that develops each individual to his highest potential.[3] Also, almost all students in the more highly developed nations will need to complete at least secondary education.

It is clear that educational planning must begin with an analysis of the social changes taking place, the new tasks and responsibilities of individuals in a changing society, and the potential for education to prepare individuals for the new society. While this is not the place to consider these long-term problems in detail, it is possible to indicate some of the new demands on education. Briefly, these are likely to emphasize some of the following goals for education:[4]

a. There must be increasing emphasis on the higher mental processes of problem-solving rather than the existing stress on information learning. Only as individuals develop skill in the more complex types of thinking will they be able to cope with the many new problems they must face in their educational and post-educational careers in a rapidly changing society.

b. There must be increasing emphasis on the basic ideas, structure, and methods of inquiry of each subject field rather than on the minutiae of the subject matter. Individuals must be able to cope with the rapidly expanding and changing body of knowledge in each field and they must be able to find the ways in which the subject fields contribute ideas and tools of thinking necessary for the larger world outside the classroom.

c. More stress must be placed on "learning to learn" than has previously been true. Each person is likely to have to relearn his own occupation a number of times during his career. Furthermore, learning must continue throughout life, if the individual is to cope with the changing nature of the society, the many new demands on him, and his own possibilities for self-actualization and fulfillment.

d. Increasing stress must be placed on those aspects of interests, attitudes, and personality which will promote the further growth of the individual, enable him to find satisfaction in the things he does, and help him to find meaning and fulfillment in his life. The effects of automation, the shorter work week, urban living, and the fast pace of change on the national as well as international scene require individual character development which will enable each person to live with himself and with others under conditions very different from those which have prevailed.

But these are the long-term changes which will require a new conception of the task of the schools, a
new orientation to teacher training and school organization, and new developments in the curriculum, teaching methods, and views about the role of the student,
the teacher, the administrator, and even parents.[5]
While we do possess some of the necessary theoretical
and practical knowledge, we shall need new knowledge
and new types of educational leadership to make these
long-term changes effectively. In the light of the
vast changes taking place, we are all culturally deprived. A new culture is rapidly emerging and the
home and the school at present do not effectively prepare the young for adaptation to and, even, survival
in this new culture.[6] This task is so great that all
of us must have some tendency to shrink from the great
demands it will place on us.

But, there is a much more immediate problem. This
is in some ways an easier problem to attack and it must
be solved in the present. We cannot wait for a decade
in which to gradually find solutions for this problem.

In the present educational system in the U.S. (and
elsewhere) we find a substantial group of students who
do not make normal progress in their school learning.
Predominantly, these are the students whose early experiences in the home, whose motivation for present
school learning, and whose goals for the future are
such as to handicap them in schoolwork. This group
may also be defined as those who do not complete secondary education. As a first estimate, we would include
the approximately one-third of the high-school entrants in the nation who do not complete secondary
school.[7] This figure is higher in many cities where
slum living and educational segregation enlarge the
problem.

It is this group with which we are at present concerned. We will refer to this group as culturally disadvantaged or culturally deprived because we believe
the roots of their problem may in large part be traced
to their experiences in homes which do not transmit the
cultural patterns necessary for the types of learning
characteristic of the schools and the larger society.

4

A large proportion of these youth come from homes in which the adults have a minimal level of education. Many of them come from homes where poverty, large family size, broken homes, discrimination, and slum conditions further complicate the picture.

While this group does include such in-migrants to the urban areas as Puerto Ricans, Mexicans, and southern-rural Negroes and whites, it also includes many individuals who were born in the large cities. It also includes many individuals living in small towns and rural areas. The designation of cultural deprivation should not be equated with membership in an ethnic group, but should be defined in terms of characteristics of the individual and/or the characteristics of his environment.[8]

Cultural deprivation should not be equated with race. It is true that a large number of Negro children, especially those from homes with functionally illiterate parents, are likely to be culturally deprived. However, it is likely that as many as one-third of the Negro children in the large cities of the U.S. are at least the equal of the white norms for educational development. It should, however, be recognized that dramatic attention to the problems of cultural deprivation has come from the civil rights movement, as well as from the rearrangement of whites and Negroes in the large cities with regard to place of residence and school attendance.

A central factor in the entire problem of education and cultural deprivation is the rapidly changing economy and job-distribution system which requires more and better education for the entire population.[9] It is this new set of requirements which force changes in education to meet the special problems of cultural deprivation in various groups in our society. In years to come, we are likely to be grateful to the civil rights movement for its contribution in bringing about much-needed educational changes. To delay these changes any longer would result in crises (disaffected youth, unemployable adults, and an economically disabled group) of even greater significance than those crises brought about more directly by the civil rights movement.

5

The task of changing the schools of the U.S. from a
selective system which rewards and finally graduates
only the more able students to one which develops each
individual to his fullest capabilities is a difficult
one. This task was started with the development of free
public education through the secondary level and the
compulsory school-attendance laws. That the schools of
the U.S. now do give opportunity for all is, with some
exceptions, generally true. The inequalities in the
opportunities for education are well established. However, what is now required is not equality of access to
education. What is needed to solve our current as well
as future crises in education is a system of compensatory education which can prevent or overcome earlier
deficiencies in the development of each individual. Essentially, what this involves is the writing and filling
of educational prescriptions for groups of children
which will enable them to realize their fullest development. Compensatory education as we understand it is
not the reduction of all education to a least common de-
nominator. It is a type of education which should help
socially disadvantaged students without reducing the
quality of education for those who are progressing sa-
tisfactorily under existing educational conditions.

It is in this context that a carefully selected
group of leaders in educational and social science research met at the University of Chicago in June, 1964.
One task this group worked on was the attempt to state
what we now know about cultural deprivation and education.

In the following sections we have attempted to state
in brief form what is now known about some of the relationships between deprivation and learning. The basis
for these statements is set forth in a series of appendix notes which the interested reader may examine in
more detail. Then, we have tried to state a general
position with respect to the responsibility for solutions to these problems. Finally, we have suggested
some of the implications of this knowledge and responsibility for the work of the schools. These implications have been formulated in a series of recommendations for the schools, the communities, as well as the
nation.

Since the school organization is at present an age-graded system, we have organized this report with respect to the critical age and developmental periods for education and cultural deprivation. We believe that this organization of the report will help those especially concerned with a particular level of education find the material most relevant to their educational problems.

Section 2

There is almost unanimous agreement that the prior
satisfaction of the so-called basic needs is necessary
before human beings can become concerned with and perform higher-level functions. With children, the adequate satisfaction of nutritional needs and the need
for sleep and rest heightens the probability of their
being able to perform competently in school situations.
Adequate living conditions, clothing, exercise, and the
availability of medical care--all contribute to the
heightened probability of increased capability in school
situations.[10]

For children of low-income families, public health
statistics generally confirm the increased incidence of
gross organ deficiencies (for example, dental problems,
defective vision, impaired hearing) as well as diseases
commonly associated with adverse economic circumstances,
such as tuberculosis. In addition, there are a variety
of illnesses of a debilitating nature that are commonly
not treated in this group and sap their energies. Included here are various specific deficiency problems
and parasitic invasions.

These deficiencies in basic needs operate to influence learning in a number of ways. Much of the energy
and attention of the child is directed to his immediate
needs and he is less able to attend to learning and
school tasks which must seem to him as less urgent and
obviously not very relevant to his present state. Even
if the child does become accustomed to a lower level of
living and to the rare feeling of well-being, he may
have such a low level of energy as to be easily fatigued
and to have relatively little endurance for the complex
and demanding tasks of learning.[11] Furthermore, the
satisfaction of immediate goals becomes more important
to these children and their parents and less energy is
available for distant goals or long-range planning. Present-time orientation becomes far more central in their
conception of things than future-time orientation--and
much of education and learning is necessarily for some
future time.

When children learn that their basic needs cannot
be adequately provided for in a dependable way, they
too often adopt a fatalistic attitude which generalizes
to alter their patterns of living. Their ability to
cope with the environment--to see light ahead--is impaired. Such passivity and defeatism (and, possibly,
hostility) stemming from need deprivation is learned
by the child from both the realities of living and from
the parents who, through their daily behavior, communicate a general attitudinal orientation. This general
attitude orientation can do much to give the child a
self-fulfilling prophecy in which he expects to be
frustrated in meeting his basic needs and in turn his
expectations determine his views about himself and his
environment. This prophecy, which is repeatedly verified, has basic consequences on personality and character.[12]

While we must not confuse biological deprivation
with cultural deprivation, there is little doubt that
very frequently the two are associated, especially in
the more poverty-stricken groups in our society. We
do wish to emphasize that meeting these physical needs
does not, by itself, lead to better learning. The adequate meeting of the basic needs merely sets the stage
for the more direct attack on the problems of learning
in this group.

Some Implications for the Schools

We do not regard the schools as having major responsibility for solving problems of poverty, but it is
clear that the schools have a responsibility in helping
school children meet these basic biological needs and
especially so when adequate school learning is partially blocked by these need deficits. In our society
parents take pride in "providing for their children"
and the permanent "taking over" of such functions by
the school or the community can have an adverse effect
on the parents' sense of adequacy. Insofar as possible,
provision for children should be made by their parents.
However, we wish to stress that the physical needs of
the children must be met and that no child should be expected to learn under conditions likely to nullify the
efforts of the teacher and the school.

9

We have listened to many anecdotes about "heroic" school principals who provided special services such as dental care, clothing, and food either on their own or in violation of school regulations. While we might applaud such efforts, we are inclined to believe that these are the exceptions and that many children must do without because there is no way in which such basic needs can be met within the present school regulations.

That children should struggle to learn under such handicaps should be regarded as a serious indictment of school regulations and community morality. No child should be permitted or expected to learn under such adverse circumstances as hunger, fatigue, disease, or impaired bodily functions. If it is the school regulations which are at fault, they must be changed. If it is the lack of food and other provisions, action at the community, state, or national level should be quick and adequate.

Recommendations

1. Each child should be assured of an adequate breakfast to help him begin the learning tasks of the day. Each child should also be assured of a mid-day meal. If these meals cannot be provided by the home, they should be provided by the school or the community in such a way that no child feels a sense of shame or special distinction.[13]

2. Each child should be given appropriate and frequent physical examinations by nurses, doctors, and dentists to deter-

mine special needs with respect to fatigue,
disease, and dental, visual, and hearing
problems. If these health services cannot be provided by the parents, it is the
responsibility of the school and the community to see that they are taken care of.

3. No child should be subjected to feelings
   of inadequacy and shame because of lack
   of necessary clothing. If these needs
   cannot be provided by the parents, it is
   the responsibility of the school and community to see that each child is adequately clothed.

Section 3

It is clear that children do not come to school equally prepared for the learning tasks of first grade. This statement will not come as a surprise to elementary-school teachers who have always had to deal with such differences. However, the research of the past decade has been of great value in helping us understand not only how the children may be different in their responsiveness to learning experiences but also how some of these differences come to be.

Until recently, differences in children's I.Q. were attributed largely to native endowment; very little of the variation was attributed to the effects of environment. The more recent research has demonstrated that for children growing up under adverse circumstances the I.Q. may be depressed by a significant amount and that intervention at certain points (and especially in the period from ages three to nine) can raise the I.Q. by as much as ten to fifteen points. Such effects have been most clearly demonstrated for children with initial I.Q.'s of less than 110. While there is nothing sacred about the I.Q., it has been a useful indicator of general learning capability in the schools. A change in I.Q. is symptomatic of a change in general learning capability and this is likely to be verified by more direct measures of school learning. Furthermore, the measurement of the culturally deprived child's intelligence at one point does not determine the upper limits of what he might be able to learn in the schools if more favorable conditions are subsequently provided in the home and/or in the school.[14]

Research reveals the aspects of the home environment which seem to be most significant in affecting the level of measured intelligence of the child as well as his school learning. In most general terms these may be described as involving provisions for general learning, models and help in language development, and parental stimulation and concern for achievement and learning on the part of the child. For the most part, it is the adults in the home who serve to stimulate the child's intellectual development.[15] Other research reveals the very early development of the child's language and cognition and the extent to which further growth takes place each year.[16]

While such empirical research does reveal some of the characteristics of the home environment which relate to and which influence the development of intelligence, it does not reveal the dynamic process by which the interaction between the child and the world about him takes place. Theoretical analyses and clinical types of investigations help to reveal something of the process by which intellectual development takes place in early childhood.

Beginning very early, the child comes to perceive many aspects in the world about him. This perceptual development takes place through the sensory modalities such as vision, hearing, touch, and even taste and smell. This development continues in more and more complex ways as the child approaches the beginning of formal schooling at age six. Perceptual development is stimulated by environments which are rich in the range of experiences available; which make use of games, toys, and many objects for manipulation; and in which there is frequent interaction between the child and adults at meals, playtimes, and throughout the day. At the beginning of the first grade there are differences between culturally deprived and culturally advantaged children in the amount and variety of experiences they have had and in their perceptual development. Although differences in perceptual development are less evident by age nine, it is likely that the differences present at age six make for differences in school learning in the first few grades. The typical middle-class home provides a very complex environment for the child's early perceptual development, and this gives these children some advantage in the early years of school.[17]

Linked to this perceptual development of the child is his linguistic development. As the child comes to perceive the world about him, he is able to "fix" or hold particular objects and events in his mind as he is given words or other symbols to "attach" to them. "Mama" and "Dadee" become representations of the important adults in his life. "Bottle," "cup," "dog," become symbols for appropriate objects in the environ-

13

ment. The adults in middle-class homes characteristically tend to use words so freely and easily that they teach them to the child at almost every opportunity. They encourage the child to say the word aloud, correct him when he, says it incorrectly or applies it to the wrong object or event, and reward him when he uses the word or symbol correctly. This corrective feedback, which seems to be essential to the learning of language in relation to experience, is more readily available to the culturally advantaged child than it is to other children.

As the child attempts to communicate with others, and especially with his parents, he uses a relatively crude and limited language. In many middle-class homes, the child's language is extended by the parent's responses to his statements and questions. In culturally deprived homes, the parent is more likely to respond to the child with a monosyllable or to nod the head without using any words. The point of this is that one major difference between culturally deprived and more advantaged homes is the extension and development of the speech of children. Such differences have become very evident as a result of the studies done in various homes where parents are observed interacting with their children.[18]

As a child develops more complex language, he becomes more able to perceive aspects of his environment, to abstract such aspects and to fix them in his memory, and to gain considerable control over his environment through the use of language. The frequent use of language in relation to his environment and the people in it enables the child to use words and language as tools for thought. Furthermore, the child becomes able to use language to express his own emotions, intentions, and desires. He is able to consider alternatives with regard to his emotions and to develop ways of delaying the gratification of his desires. Finally, the child develops his ability to compare, differentiate, and abstract aspects of his environment as well as his own thoughts and emotions.[19] Here again the child in the culturally advantaged home is given a great deal of opportunity to use language in these more complex ways, while the child in the disadvantaged home has less opportunity to develop in this way.

14

Put in other terms, the child in many middle-class homes is given a great deal of instruction about the world in which he lives, to use language to fix aspects of this world in his memory, and to think about similarities, differences, and relationships in this very complex environment. Such instruction is individual and is timed in relation to the experiences, actions, and questions of the child. Parents make great efforts to motivate the child, to reward him, and to reinforce desired responses. The child is read to, spoken to, and is constantly subjected to a stimulating set of experiences in a very complex environment. In short, he "learns to learn" very early. He comes to view the world as something he can master through a relatively enjoyable type of activity, a sort of game, which is learning. In fact, much of the approval he gets is because of his rapid and accurate response to this informal instruction in the home.

"Learning to learn" should not be confused with the early teaching of the child to read, to spell, and even to do simple arithmetic. Such coaching in the home is merely trying to do the school's task before the child enters public education. "Learning to learn" is a far more basic type of learning than coaching the child on school learning. It includes motivating the child to find pleasure in learning. It involves developing the child's ability to attend to others and to engage in purposive action. It includes training the child to delay the gratification of his desires and wishes and to work for rewards and goals which are more distant. It includes developing the child's view of adults as sources of information, and ideas, and also as sources of approval and reward. Through such development the child changes his self-expectations and his expectations of others.[20]

While all of this is not absent in the culturally deprived home, it does not play such a central role in child rearing in such homes. The size of the family, the concern of the parents with the basic necessities of life, the low level of educational development of the parents, the frequent absence of a male parent, and the lack of a great deal of interaction between children and adults all conspire to reduce the stimulation, language development, and intellectual development of such children.[21]

If the home does not and cannot provide these basic developments, the child is likely to be handicapped in much of his later learning and the prognosis for his educational development is very poor. Such a child is likely to have difficulty and to be constantly frustrated by the demands of the typical elementary-school program. His frustrations and disappointments in school are likely to have an adverse effect on his view of himself and his main desire must be to escape from the virtual imprisonment which school comes to represent for him.[22]

Implications for the Schools

Ideally, the early intellectual development of the child should take place in the home. Some efforts have been made to help parents learn how to teach their children. Under some conditions this is likely to be fruitful. But we must express pessimism about such possibilities when the total syndrome of poverty, broken homes, slum living, large families, and illiteracy all conspire against the intellectual development of the child. To point out the small number of exceptional children who are able to overcome these handicaps is not to prove that these conditions have no effect: it is to demonstrate the rarity of the exceptions to the general effects of cultural deprivation.

All later learning is likely to be influenced by the very basic learning which has taken place by the age of five or six. If adequate basic learning cannot be provided in the home, it is the responsibility of the schools to insure that the culturally deprived children have as good a set of initial skills and intellectual development as children from more culturally advantaged homes. This position may be taken in the interest of the individual child. But also, this position may be taken to insure that the work of the schools for the next ten years will not be largely wasted because of what has taken place in the previous two or three years. Careful studies in the U.S. and other countries demonstrate that it is possible to bring culturally deprived children up to satisfactory stages of readiness for the regular school learning.[23] If this can be done on a broader base, then the regular learning procedures of the schools which are now quite

16

effective for the advantaged children are also likely
to be effective for the culturally disadvantaged children.

While we would advocate that the intellective training of the child be done in the home and by the parents,
if they cannot do it adequately, the school is the
logical social agency to do it.

Recommendations

1. Nursery schools and kindergartens should
    be organized to provide culturally de-
    prived children with the conditions for
    their intellectual development and the
    learning-to-learn stimulation which is
    found in the most favorable home environ-
    ments.

Such nursery schools and kindergartens should be
very different from the nursery schools and kindergartens commonly used for middle-class children. These
nursery schools and kindergartens must systematically
provide for the intellectual development of the child.
Much learning can take place through games, concrete
materials (blocks, toys, objects), and dramatic play.
The adult teachers must provide a supportive structured environment in which being read to, music, and
art are enjoyable social experiences for the children.
Specifically, the primary task of these nursery schools
and kindergartens should be to provide for:[24]

a. Stimulation of children to perceive aspects of the
    world about them and to fix these aspects by the
    use of language.

b. Development of more extended and accurate language.

c. Development of a sense of mastery over aspects of
    the immediate environment and an enthusiasm for
    learning for its own sake.

17

d. Development of thinking and reasoning and the
    ability to make new insights and discoveries for
    oneself.

e. Development of purposive learning activity and the
    ability to attend for longer periods of time.

2. A national commission composed of teach-
    ers and other specialists should be crea-
    ted to co-ordinate and to develop curri-
    cular guidelines, materials, and methods
    for this special type of nursery school-
    kindergarten.

    This commission should be charged with responsi-
    bility for experimenting with alternative approaches
    to these problems and for evaluating the effectiveness
    of such curricula with different groups of children.

3. The teachers for this new type of nursery
    school-kindergarten should be carefully
    trained for the very specific set of
    tasks they must assume. Essentially,
    these teachers should be trained to do
    for many children what very good parents
    can do for a small number of their own
    children.

    There is an urgency about this problem and it is
    likely that some of the training will have to be done
    while the teachers are actually in the schools. Volun-
    teer workers (including parents) and adolescent assist-
    ants could do much to provide the necessary conditions
    for learning in these nursery school-kindergartens.

4. The parents must be sufficiently involved in the nursery school-kindergarten to understand its importance for their child and to give support and reinforcement to the tasks of these special schools. The parents should be so committed to this type of school that they are willing to do everything possible to insure the continuity of the child's school experiences.

Ideally, the parents should learn the appropriate communication patterns so that they can do much of this on their own with their own children. One might foresee the time when most parents can provide such stimulating home environments for the development of their children that special nursery school-kindergartens will not be widely needed. To this end, every effort should be made to have parents serve as part-time assistants and observers in these schools.

Section 4

During the past three decades there has been a tremendous influx into the large cities of children who do not seem able to take advantage of the educational opportunities offered by the conventional elementary school. Methods and materials which have served the average child well do not seem to help the culturally disadvantaged child acquire the vital communication and computation skills which are so necessary to achievement of educational goals. Conventional approaches to the acquiring of these skills make learning demands on disadvantaged children which they simply are not able to meet. The gaps between the learning tasks and the "readiness" of the children are a source of frustration to the teachers as well as the children. All too quickly, the teacher and the child are ready to give up the struggle--both with a terrible sense of being defeated.[25]

As was pointed out in the previous section, the culturally deprived child comes to school with deficits in learning sets and the ability to "learn to learn." Since he lacks particular experiences and since he is at a relatively low level of linguistic development, he is usually not ready to begin his learning at the same level and by the same approach as is characteristic of children from favorable cultural environments. Unless the school reshapes its curriculum and methods to begin with the child where he is, learning cannot proceed in a fruitful and meaningful way.

Present school practices do not succeed in overcoming the initial differences between culturally advantaged and culturally disadvantaged children. Instead, what start as small measurable differences in the first grade become larger each year. By the end of the sixth year of school, there is a cumulative deficit in the school achievement of the culturally disadvantaged children which shows up most clearly in the tool subjects of reading and arithmetic. But, even in the measures of general intelligence many of these children appear to decline during the period of grade 1 to grade 6. It is this cumulative deficit which must be reversed as early as possible in the culturally deprived child's school career.[26]

The child from the culturally deprived home comes to school with an interest in the new experiences but without some of the experiences, skills, and values typical of the middle-class child. The culturally advantaged child has been amply rewarded for his previous learning, and he is likely to begin school valuing achievement (and specifically school achievement) as a good in its own right. In contrast, the culturally deprived child has difficulty in learning for its own sake and in learning for the approval of an adult. He values things and activities which are concrete and which have immediate and tangible rewards. He has difficulty in seeing the relevance of much of school learning since he is unable to comprehend fully or accept the deferred and symbolic gratification that the middle-class child has come to accept.[27] As each year of school goes by, the culturally disadvantaged child suffers further frustration and failure. He is rarely rewarded or approved in the school and is penalized and disapproved of more strongly each year. As this increasing failure becomes apparent to the child and to all who are concerned with him (parents, teachers, school administrators), the child becomes alienated from the school program. He recognizes that there is little likelihood that he will get satisfaction from his schoolwork and he seeks satisfying experiences elsewhere. He usually turns to his peers for more satisfying relations than he has with adults. For this as well as for other reasons, the peer group becomes more central in the life of lower-class children far earlier than it does for middle-class children.

The culturally deprived child has some special difficulties because the school learning environment and materials are so very different from the settings which are familiar to him. However, it is in the reduced physical activity of the school and in the demand for long spans of attention that he is at a special disadvantage as compared with children from culturally advantaged homes. It is difficult for him to learn to be quiet and to attend to a flow of words (many of which he does not understand) from the teacher.

21

The elementary school teacher is expected to use the conventional materials and methods of the elementary school curriculum for all children. As the teacher becomes frustrated because of the relatively poor progress of the culturally disadvantaged children, she is likely to place the blame on the children (or their parents) rather than on the curriculum and methods of instruction. The discouragement of the teacher is communicated to the children. Finally, the teacher faced with restless children learning poorly views her task as primarily one of maintaining discipline and order. Teacher and child alike seek ways of getting out of what has come to be a bad situation for both.[28] While it is possible for the teachers and school administrators to blame the home and the parents for the difficulties these children have in learning, this placement of blame does little good for the child or the teacher who must deal with him. Furthermore, this placement of blame does little to attack the central problem which is the improvement of the learning of the child as early as possible in his school career.

The first three years of the elementary school are critical. If learning is not successful and satisfying in these years, the entire educational career of the child is seriously jeopardized. The child's interest in school learning, the problems of the school dropout, and the educational and vocational career of the individual are largely determined by what takes place in the first few years of public school.[29]

Even more serious than the lack of effective conventional school learning is the effect of continuous failure on the child's image of himself and his attitude toward others. It is a serious blow to one's pride to suffer failure time and time again. Success gives one courage to attempt more and more complex tasks--failure does not.[30]

Some Implications for the Schools

Since the present introductory years of the elementary school do not effectively prepare the culturally deprived child for the later years of school, it is the clear responsibility of the schools to devise a more effective school program for these children.

The development of a more effective school program
for these children can do much to help them solve the
learning tasks of the school and at the same time acquire a more adequate self-image. It is in the interest of the school to halt the cumulative deficits of
these children as early as possible in order to make
later instruction and learning increasingly effective.
Ideally, a solution to the learning problems of these
children in the first few grades of elementary school
should mean that the existing school programs at later
grades are likely to become more effective, and there
will be less need for drastic modification of these
school curricula.

It would be most efficient and effective if the
early learning in the home prepared these children for
the elementary school. Where the home cannot provide
this preparation, it would be in the interests of the
child and the school if this could be done during the
nursery school-kindergarten period. If circumstances
prevent these solutions or attacks on the problem, then
the earlier in the elementary school that appropriate
school programs are made available to these children,
the better for all concerned.

There is increasing evidence that elementary school
programs have been developed which reduce the cumulative
deficits in learning. Some of these school programs appear to have such powerful effects in the improvement of
reading, language (including speech), and arithmetic
that the differences between culturally disadvantaged
and culturally advantaged children become very small.[31]

The schools must recognize the complexity of the
educational problem of these children and must not expect to solve these problems by some single change such
as a new textbook, a more favorable teacher-pupil ratio,
a teaching machine, etc. The basic problem is to start
with the child where he is and to proceed by a carefully
developed and sequential program to bring him up to a
level where he can learn as well as other children and
eventually under the same conditions as other children.

If an effective program of nursery school and kindergarten education has already been established, there
should be less need for marked changes in the methods

and curriculum of the elementary school. The following recommendations are made on the assumption that the majority of culturally deprived children still begin school at Grade 1 and that this will be true for some time to come.

Recommendations

1. Evidence should be obtained on each child at the beginning of the first grade to determine the levels he has reached with regard to perceptual development, language development, ability to attend, and motivation for learning.

Such evidence may be obtained by the use of previous records and special tests as well as by observing the child in actual learning situations for several weeks. On the basis of this evidence, an educational prescription should be written for the child and he should be placed with others in an appropriate section with a teacher who can best provide what he needs.[32]

2. In each school, there should be a number of approaches to introductory learning, and each child should be placed in the approach which is most appropriate for him.

Some of these approaches might stress early learning and readiness, others could stress an experience approach to language and reading; and, still others might stress the present regular programs of reading and arithmetic. Ideally, each teacher should become a specialist in a particular approach to learning as well as a specialist in dealing with a particular range of learning problems.

Since these first years are so important, these should be the years in which each teacher has the smallest number of children (preferably less than 20); each teacher should be aided by specialists in speech, reading, and school psychology; and each teacher should be aided by a pool of curriculum materials, games, self-learning devices, and other learning materials. The use of teaching aids and assistants can do much to improve the effectiveness of instruction in these grades.

3. The emphasis in the first three years of elementary school should be on the development of each child with careful evaluation records of his progress toward clear-cut tasks and goals. In these years, the child should not be failed or expected to repeat a grade or year. The careful sequential development of each child must be one of continual success at small tasks.[33]

4. A national commission of teachers and other specialists should be created to co-ordinate and to develop the curricular guidelines, materials, and methods for the first three years of elementary school for culturally deprived children. This commission should develop several alternative approaches to the problem and should

evaluate the effectiveness of such curricula.

Much of the initial work of this commission may be to appraise the effectiveness of some of the promising approaches already being used in some of the schools in large cities.

5. The teaching staff for the first three years of school should be carefully selected and should have many opportunities for in-service education on the curriculum problems of these years. They should be so organized that they can provide continuity and sequential development for each child. They should regard their central task as helping each child master the fundamental skills in language, reading, and arithmetic as well as develop a general skill in learning itself.

The teachers must be free to try new approaches to these goals and should regard themselves as the key persons in helping each child create the base on which the entire educational (and vocational) future of the individual depends. Salary, status, and training should be commensurate with this great responsibility.

6. Since the home is so important in the work of the schools--especially in the elementary school period--every effort

must be made to strengthen the relation

between the home and the school. Parents

must be involved in such a way that they

can understand the importance of this

level of schooling and so that they can

provide support and reinforcement for the

learning tasks of the school. Both teach-

ers and parents must come to understand

the ways in which the learning progress

of all children is a dual task involving

home and school.

The schools must find ways of involving parents by
imaginative devices such as special tutoring by the more
able parents. Most central is the recognition by teachers and parents of the role of the parents in raising
the aspirations of children and in the valuing of education and learning as a major means of gaining security
and mobility.[34]

It is hoped that the involvement of the home and
appropriate changes in school district regulations[35] to
reduce pupil transfers will do much to increase the continuity of relationship between each child and his teacher. This continuity is important in insuring sequence
of learning and the establishment of the necessary human
relationships for effective learning.

7. For culturally disadvantaged children who

have not had the benefits of a revised

curriculum in the first years of school

there should be an all out effort to halt

the cumulative deficits in learning achievement at the later grades. While this is likely to be increasingly difficult as the child gets older, every resource should be available to the teachers at these levels. If it is necessary to sacrifice some aspects of the curriculum in order to bring these children to higher levels of achievement, the emphasis should be on the language development of the child, reading, and arithmetic.

A longer school day, summer programs, small group instruction, teacher assistants and tutoring programs, the aid of specialists, the use of diagnostic instruments, and the development of more effective instructional materials for this age group should all contribute to the educational development of these children.[36]

Special Case of the Negro Student

The Negro child who is culturally deprived has all
the learning problems of other culturally deprived
children. However, in addition to these problems he
suffers from the special problems created by the preju-
dices and attitudes of others.

For 100 years, the major economic and cultural de-
terrents to achievement in school on the part of Negro
students--and they are tragically destructive forces--
have been, and still remain those described below.

The organized system of economic, political, and
educational subordination of Negroes, both in the South
and in the North, has systematically barred Negroes
from skilled or white-collar jobs in business, industry, or government. For generations, an economic
blockade has been maintained against Negroes, with the
result that most of them felt that there was nothing
to be gained by being educated. Most of those who obtained an education found no openings except in teaching in Negro schools, and in the U. S. Postal Service.
A very few worked in Negro insurance companies or small
businesses. (Except for the tiny group of Negro phy-
sicians and dentists, this was the entire educated Negro middle class 20 years ago.)

The system of segregated schools has meant inferior
education for Negro children. The system of political
disfranchisement in the South has supported the whole
system of oppression and subordination. Without the
vote, Negroes have not been able to protect themselves
against political and legalized exploitation. They
have not had the chance to participate as officeholders
in their own government, nor even to hold clerical jobs
in city and state departments, in the South, and in the
vast majority of Northern towns and cities.

This system has resulted in crippling economic handicaps for the families of Negro pupils. In 1962, 60
per cent of all non-white families in the United States
had incomes under $4,000, while only 26 per cent of
white families were in this lowest income group. Ac-

cording to the standards defined by the Committee on
Economic Development, at least 85 per cent of the Negro
families of the deep South, from which most Negro migrants come, have incomes which place them in the bottom
economic group, the most severely deprived. Their daily
concern is with being able to provide food and housing
for their children and themselves. They must be interested primarily in short-term goals, for their economic
life has no security; food and shelter are on a week to
week, or a month to month, basis.

Education and preparing for a skilled job or a profession, however, are long-term goals. One must have
some economic security or stability, if one is to hope
to finish high school and college. It takes at least
16 years of education to become a teacher, and usually
more to become a high-school teacher or a principal.
Economic deprivation inevitably weakens the interest of
most Negro families and children in striving for the
long-term goals of education.

The third deterrent to school achievement by the
masses of Negro children is the cultural deprivation
which results from segregation and from the poverty and
lack of educational stimulus in the home. This cultural handicap includes the lack of books, lack of emphasis on reading in the home, the dialect the child
learns from his family, and the level of parental interest in education.

There is a wonderful zest and expressiveness among
young Negro children from low economic levels. In the
schools, however, the Negro child from low economic
groups is likely to lose his expressiveness and zest
after he finishes kindergarten, unless he has a very in-
sightful and skilled teacher. He is likely to lack confidence in his ability and in his future. His parents
usually do not encourage him to compete in school, so
that he usually lacks the drive for achievement, which
is the prime incentive that middle-class parents seek
to teach their children.

Within the school itself the poor relationship between teachers and pupils, the use of tests for purposes
of classification rather than diagnosis, the primers and
readers, and the curriculum as a whole soon damage se-

verely the confidence and the basic self-esteem of the
child from low socio-economic groups. Finally, his
subordinate place in the school, as in society, tends
to weaken his self-esteem. This self-depreciation is
typical of all low-status groups and is the result of
their being stigmatized in most relationships with dominant groups, including teachers. It results not only
in a poor self-image, but often in self-contempt be-
neath the mask of hostility and resentment which the
pupil shows to the teacher.[37]

Implications for the Schools

It is when the negative attitudes and feelings of
individuals are translated into institutional practices
(school, social welfare agencies, churches, police and
courts, business and industry) that the Negro (or any
other group) most despairs. Under these conditions
there can be no hope or optimism about the future and
little incentive to work for distant goals.[38]

We do not regard the school as the agency for the
solution of the social ills of a society. However, we
do regard the schools as providing a setting in which
all can learn under as nearly ideal conditions as possible. Furthermore, the school is responsible not only
for the learning of subject matter and intellectual
skills, but also for the learning of basic attitudes and
values.

There is considerable evidence that teachers (both
white and Negro) respond differentially to white and
Negro children as well as to children of different social classes.[39] We regard such differential treatment
as harmful to the learning of the child as well as harmful to his own self-perception.

Recommendations

The recommendations throughout this report apply
to culturally deprived children of all races and ethnic
groups. In addition, the following recommendations apply to all children but are especially relevant for
Negro children for the reasons indicated in this section.

1. Especially in the early years of school
   all children must learn under the most
   positive set of human interactions. Where
   possible, teachers should be chosen because of their ability to help young children and because they can be warm and supportive to all children.

   In-service training in human relations may be of
   some help to teachers working with children coming from
   home and social backgrounds different from those of the
   teacher. These children need, most of all teachers who
   will encourage them to try, to believe in their future,
   and to believe in their abilities. They are hungry for
   encouragement, for some reason to have confidence in
   themselves against the dead weight of social and economic pressures which drive them down to self-depreciation and sullen resentment.

2. Integration will contribute most effectively to better attitudes and relations
   when there are a great variety of ways
   in which children of both races engage
   in common activities on a one-to-one basis.[40] Such attitudes and relations are
   basic to the development of our society.
   Furthermore, integration will have little
   effect on cognitive learning unless the
   basic learning needs of the children are
   met by appropriate sequential patterns

32

of learning experiences.[41] (See earlier
recommendations.)

3. With very rapid changes in the civil
    rights movement and its effect on occu-
    pational opportunities, Negro students
    must have up-to-date occupational informa-
    tion. Also, they will need more educa-
    tional and vocational guidance than other
    students. It is recommended that begin-
    ning with secondary school, Negro stu-
    dents have periodic interviews with ca-
    pable guidance workers who thoroughly
    understand the current occupational pic-
    ture. Such guidance workers should also
    have job placement functions for these
    students.

Section 6

The adolescent period is the period in which the individual attempts to create a new identity for himself and this is a period when he is especially open to new experiences which will help him determine who he is and what he might become. This is the period in which the peer group becomes very important in the life of the individual while the parents and other adults become less central than they were. This is also the period in which the individual looks to the future to determine what are the realities ahead for him and what he must do to prepare for these realities as he perceives them.

If the individual regards higher education as appropriate and available for him, his learning at the adolescent level proceeds relatively smoothly. If he does not hope and aspire for higher education and sees no relevance of secondary education for his occupational future, he "marks time" until he is permitted to drop out of school or until he completes secondary education—if pressed hard to do so.

By the beginning of secondary school, the typical culturally disadvantaged student is reading at a level approximately 3½ years below grade level. He is considerably retarded in arithmetic and other school subjects. His problem solving and abstract thinking is at a very low level as compared with others at this grade or age level. For these students there is a disaffection with school such that the student approaches learning tasks in a most apathetic manner.[42]

There is little participation in the extracurricular activities of the school other than athletics. Indeed, it would appear that most of the school activities are attractive primarily for the college-bound student.[43]

Few of the culturally deprived students at the secondary level have clear vocational goals or the motivation to persist in a learning program which may enable them to make vocational choices.[44]

34

Combined with these deficits in learning and motivation, many of these students have developed a level
of hostility and rebellion against school authorities,
teachers, and other adults which interferes with learning and which makes their own lives one of continual
resentment against individuals and forces around them.

The culturally disadvantaged student has all too
frequently given up hope for the future. Frustrated
by the school's demands and by its repeated punishment
(and lack of rewards), he sees little relevance in
present school learning for the realities he perceives
ahead. All that is interesting and meaningful at this
stage is his membership in a peer society which finds
no place for itself in the school.

The peer society provides for many lower-class
youth a very exciting and rewarding life. Such a society enables him to become relatively independent of
adult control. In such a society he has opportunities
for becoming a leader or for participating in significant activities under leaders he admires and with others
who share a common set of interests and values. The
peer society frequently provides relationships between
girls and boys at a level of intensity far beyond that
approved by adults or social institutions like the
school, church, or community organizations. Put in
other terms, the school with its emphasis on learning
tasks, deferred gratifications, and adult-controlled
social activity has a difficult time in competing with
a peer society which offers exciting and meaningful activity with immediate and powerful rewards quite independent of adult controls.

The secondary school system has functioned as a selective system giving its major attention to the youth
who are able to complete it successfully and priding
itself primarily on the youth who are in college preparatory programs. The schools have not been able to
find ways of reaching in a very vital way approximately
one-third of the youth who begin secondary education.

It is the establishment of one's identity which is
undoubtedly the central developmental task of adolescence. The individual is beginning to make a balance
sheet of the negative and positive aspects of his per-

sonality and character. He sees himself as somewhat
alienated and different from his parents and is groping
for models of persons who best combine the characteristics he admires. He would like to become more like
these models and he begins to imitate some of the more
superficial characteristics of these models, that is,
dress, appearance, and mannerisms. He is also desper-
ately searching for a set of values and attitudes which
will give meaning to his life and which will make him a
unique individual who has worth in his own eyes, and
perhaps in the eyes of others. Finally, he (or she) is
seeking to establish his own adequacy as a male or female in our society. This definition of adequacy involves attractiveness to members of the opposite sex as
well as adequacy as a male or female in the eyes of
members of his (or her) own sex. In our society this
sense of adequacy is also related to being able to enter a vocation (or marriage) which will give him sufficient material resources to enable him to lead at
least as good a life as his parents. For some, this
notion of a vocation includes satisfaction in the work,
status, and the opportunity to contribute to others.[45]

As one views the problems of the adolescent, and
especially those of the culturally disadvantaged adolescent, against the present organization and curriculum of the schools, it becomes clear that the schools
are not meeting the special needs of this group. This
occurs partly because the school is only one of the social institutions in the community which has a sense of
responsibility for this group, and all too frequently
these different social institutions have no way of working together on a common set of problems. In part, also,
the schools and the other social institutions are working in traditional ways while the larger society--the
city, the economy, and the government--is changing so
rapidly that traditional approaches to the problem are
no longer adequate. Finally, the core of the over-all
problem is that a rapidly changing society raises questions about traditional values, as does the adolescent
society, and there are no simple ways for developing a
new set of values quickly.

Implications for the Schools (and Community)

The schools working alone can do a great deal for

36

some culturally disadvantaged adolescents. Working alone, the schools can do somewhat less for a sizeable portion of this group. Only as the schools combine their efforts with the efforts of other community agencies and cooperate with industry and government can the problems facing the majority of these adolescents be effectively solved.

In a society which has need for a constantly increasing portion of its youth to secure higher education, some more concerted effort must be made to enable a larger portion of these youth to secure higher education. In the culturally disadvantaged group there is a sizeable proportion of the youth (perhaps one-third) who can aspire to higher education and who should be enabled to secure this higher education.

Recommendations

1. A major effort must be made to identify, by the beginning of secondary education, a sizeable group of deprived students who can with appropriate continual effort on the part of the school be enabled to complete secondary education successfully and begin higher education. These students must be offered special instructional programs, tutorial help as needed, increased counseling, and help on the basic skills and tool subjects (for example, Higher Horizons Project).[46]

It is quite possible that these students could, by a system of tutoring less able students, be able to satisfy their own needs for service to others and at the same time begin to make their own aspirations for higher

37

education more realistic. (Thus, a system of remuneration for tutoring other students including the younger students could be supported by the state and national government so that each year the student from the 9th through the 12th grade could receive some pay while an equal amount was put in a special higher education fund to be made available when he entered a higher educational institution.) The point of all this is that each individual needs to make real his aspirations for the future while at the same time he needs to have a sense of independence as well as a sense of dedication and service to others. Such a system of earning his way by tutoring others could remove the stigma of being a special recipient of philanthropy or charity.

2. Culturally disadvantaged adolescents who are having great difficulty with the regular school curricula should have a school program which emphasizes the basic skills of language and reading and they should be permitted to specialize in an area in which they are especially interested.

Such a program would reduce the emphasis on general education courses and would permit the student to go as far as he can go in some area of specialization. Such specialization could begin as early as the 9th year of school.

It is especially important for these students to have a detailed diagnosis of their special weaknesses and strengths in the basic skills and be helped by appropriate remedial measures, tutorial instruction, and more effective curricular materials.

3. For these youth, there should be work-study plans in which students can learn in relation to the work. This requires

very effective co-operation between
schools, industry, and public agencies.[47]

Work on blind-alley positions which involve little
opportunity for learning would have little value for
the student. It is quite possible that work-study
programs could be developed in which the type of work
experiences are arranged in an increasing order of complexity from jobs that could be learned in a single
week to jobs that require many weeks to master. If
then, students could begin with simple jobs, learn
them and then move to more complex jobs, they could
develop some of the basic abilities of learning to
work and learning to adapt to different work situations. Ideally, a student might have four to six work
experiences during the age period 16 to 19. A student
in these work experiences should be appropriately su-
pervised and helped to learn both on the job and in the
school. The student should be moved to as complex a
type of work as he can master and increasingly his
work experiences should be related to the types of
jobs for which there will be greatest need in industry
and the community. Students in these work-study plans
will need frequent counseling in order to understand
the realities of the job market in relation to their
own skills and expectations. A specially trained group
of counselors will be needed to help these students
with their educational-vocational decisions.

4. For all youth, and especially for the cul-

    turally disadvantaged youth, there should

    be peer societies which have continuity

    over the age period 14-19 and which pro-

    vide opportunities for social relations,

    service to others, and the development of

    meaningful value patterns. Such peer

    societies may be organized by appropriate

39

community agencies with the co-operation

of the schools.

This type of peer society requires much more than
the present type of extracurricular and social activities of the high school which do not at present have a
place for lower-class youth.

In these peer societies there must be a place for
key adult personalities in the community. This type
of peer society plays a major role in other countries
and provides the youth with a meaningful set of relationships and activities. Associated with the peer
society should be opportunities for counseling youth,
recreational activities, and facilities for group meetings. Ideally, the peer society should enable youth to
find support and help from others at a most critical
stage in their lives.

Appendix Notes

Section 1

1.   Buckingham (1962, p. 165) in a symposium on education and automation noted: "Less than half of U. S. employers will even consider hiring a high school dropout. Furthermore, the dropout, if hired, is the first fired, is the lowest paid, and has the least chance for advancement. Roughly 18 per cent of our unskilled workers are now unemployed. This is about double the rate for semiskilled workers. Eighty per cent of those now unemployed did not finish high school."

Schreiber (1964a, p. 2) states that "the essential problem has . . . to do . . . with the fact that the world to which contemporary dropouts seek entrance has a diminishing place for them." Tyler (1963, p. 2) cites Bureau of Labor statistics which indicate that " . . . not only is a high school education essential for most employment, but the percentage of jobs requiring persons with a college education is increasing at a rapid rate." Wolfbein (1964) summarizes current employment trends in the U. S. which show decreasing job opportunities for unskilled workers.

2.   For detailed treatment of economic and social forces affecting education in the United States see: NSSE Yearbook (1961), particularly chapters by Schultz, and Bernert and Nam.

Tyler (1963) discusses the basic facts of social change which accompany the increasing use of science and technology and the implications for education.

3.   Gardner (1961) states that "what we must reach for is a conception of perceptual self discovery, perpetual reshaping to realize one's best self, to be the person one could be."

See Robbins (1963) for a good summary of British aims and principles of higher education.

41

These include preparation for the labor market, promotion of general powers of the mind, advancement of learning, and transmission of a common culture and common standards of citizenship.

4.   For discussions of new goals for education see: Bruner (1960), Thelen (1960), and Guilford (1963). For a collection of essays on aims of education by such well-known writers as Conant, Lippman, and Dewey, see Callahan (1960).

5.   For a comprehensive treatment of innovation in education see Miles (1964). The problems of curriculum development in a rapidly changing society are discussed by B. S. Bloom (1964b).

6.   Miles (1964) notes several factors presumably responsible for the "climate of urgency and accelerated educational change." Among these are struggles for national survival, demands of an affluent society for intellectually sophisticated manpower, unemployment at semi-skilled and unskilled levels, and increase in cultural and aesthetic activities. In addition, he cites the profound influence of size and growth of the educational system.

Goodman (1964) discusses the necessity of education for leisure which is radically different from present educational efforts.

C. P. Snow's (1959) discussion of the scientific revolution and the resulting educational problems includes a treatment of British, American, and Russian attempts to cope with the problem.

7.   1959 statistics showed that for all young people 14-17 years old in public schools (73 per cent of the age group), 60 per cent graduated from high school on schedule. These figures are drawn from U. S. Office of Education (1959, p. 5).

In the 1961-62 school year, 69.6 per cent of ninth graders four years earlier graduated from high school. See American Council on Education (1964, p. 266).

8. Deutsch (1963) suggests a number of character-istics of the underprivileged environment in-cluding overcrowding, substandard housing, lack of sanitary facilities, restriction to immediate environment, scarcity of toys and creative materials, and restricted verbal com-munication.

Bernstein (1962) discusses differences in family structure and activities which relate to particular types of language usage and de-velopment.

Harrington (1962) describes various poverty-stricken groups in the U. S. and the condi-tions under which they live.

Dave (1963) has found a significant relation between home environmental factors and achieve-ment in school.

See also Riessman (1962), Hunt (1964), and Davis (1948) for definitions and analyses of cultural deprivation.

9. The changing job market and its requirements has been analyzed by many writers. See, for example, Evans and Arnstein (1962), Watson (1963), and Miles (1964). Wolfbein (1964) gives statistics on the labor force patterns and trends, changing industrial and occupa-tional patterns, job mobility, unemployment, and rising educational requirements of the labor market. See also Appendix Notes 1 and 2.

Section 2

10. Maslow (1954) discusses several basic needs in terms of a hierarchy in which the physiologi-cal needs must be satisfied before the desire

43

to know and understand, as well as aesthetic needs will emerge.

Schorr (1964) suggests that "the attitudes associated with the culture of poverty--passivity, cynicism, orientation to the present-- are a realistic response to the facts of poverty." He discusses the effects of malnutrition and inadequate housing on attitudes and behavior.

See also Prescott (1958) and Havighurst and Neugarten (1962).

11. The effects of physical deprivation, such as lack of nutrition, on outlook and attitudes are not very well documented. However, there are studies of adults and children during war time which indicate loss of energy, lack of ability to concentrate, loss of self-control and increased irritability. An excellent review of these studies dealing with nutrition and its effect on growth, behavior, and mental performance has been done by Breckenridge and Vincent (1962). See, also, Keys (1950).

12. See Oscar Lewis (1959) for case studies of five Mexican families in the culture of poverty. Also, Schorr (1964) and Davis (1948) who discuss psychological effects of poverty.

13. Provision of meals for school children is a common practice in many countries. In some countries, meals are available to all children regardless of the financial status of the family (for example, Denmark, Finland, Dominican Republic). In other countries, meals are provided and ability of the family is considered; many children receive meals at little or no cost (for example, Japan, Scotland, England). See UNESCO (1955, 1958) for a comprehensive survey of these facilities in the nations of the world.

14.   Data on the effects of environment on intelligence come largely from projects aimed at providing improved environments for learning. Such projects have included mentally retarded children and children from deprived homes. They include studies of the effects of short-term learning task training and extended preschool experiences. See, as examples, Brazziel and Terrell (1962); Gray and Klaus (1963); Kirk (1958); and Smilansky (1964). In addition, Lee (1951) and Klineberg (1935) have shown increases in IQ's of children who have moved from rural south to city environments.

In addition to results of intervention programs, research shows that conditions of test administration including motivational aspects, rapport, and other factors depress the intelligence test performance of culturally deprived children. See, as illustrative, Davis (1948); Eells (1951); Douvan (1956); Haggard (1954); Klugman (1944); and Deutsch, Fishman, et al. (1964).

15.   See Dave (1963); Hunt (1961); John (1963), Milner (1951), and Wolf (1964).

16.   For a summary of the longitudinal research findings on the development of selected characteristics, see B. S. Bloom (1964a), especially chapters 3 and 4 dealing with intelligence and achievement data.

17.   Research tends to show that the home and early environment of the culturally deprived child produces certain deficits in perceptual skills. Although there is still great need for investigation in this area, it is clear that middle-class children receive more visual discriminative experience at home and that auditory discrimination of speech patterns is more highly developed. Jensen (1965) reviews work both on animals and hu-

mans on this point. See, also, Hunt (1964),
especially pages 237-239, Weaver (1963) and
Deutsch (1963).

18.   Research on language development points to
        important differences between middle-class
        and deprived children. The role of feedback
        in language development has been investigated
        by Casler (1961), John (1963), and Deutsch
        (1964a). Hess (1964a) finds marked differ-
        ences between social classes in maternal
        teaching styles. Bernstein (1961, 1962) has
        investigated different linguistic codes and
        has demonstrated relationships between these
        codes and the status systems of families.
        This research on language points to a defin-
        ite lack of preparation of deprived children
        to deal with language as it is used in school
        and to use language as an aid in conceptual-
        izing the world.

19.   Language and its effects on perception,
        thought, and behavior has been studied in
        terms of the nature of language and linguis-
        tics as well as by clinical and experimental
        approaches to the language development of the
        child during the early years. See the work
        of Carroll (1960), Luria (1960), Vigotsky
        (1962). This work has been summarized by
        Jensen (1965) and Berlyne (1963).

20.   Harlow (1949) originally used the term "learn-
        ing to learn" in his studies of learning sets.
        Although we do not use the term in the iden-
        tical sense, the centrality of past experience
        and the importance of practice apply in both
        conceptions. In our conception, the "learn-
        ing to learn" aspects of development include,
        among others, the incorporation of a reward
        system compatible with delay, a future-time
        perspective, adequate attention span, the
        valuing of educational endeavors, and the
        ability to use adults as resources. There is
        considerable research which shows that de-
        prived children are less likely to develop
        these "learning to learn" behaviors and con-

sequently will not be adequately prepared for the usual school curriculum. For research dealing with these variables, see: Davis (1944); Deutsch (1964c); Gray and Klaus (1963); Haggard (1954); Hess (1964a) LeShan (1952) Lott and Lott (1963); Mischel (1961); Rosen (1956) and Smilansky (1961).

21.   See Ausubel (1963); Deutsch (1963); Deutsch and Brown (1964); Keller (1963); Milner (1951); and Goldberg (1963).

22.   Teachers who work with deprived children report that the children experience frustration and often become apathetic or rebellious in school when they cannot succeed at the curricular tasks. Smilansky (1961) reports that ratings of deprived children after first grade show marked decreases in initiative, concentration, responsiveness to adult teachers, and effectiveness of work habits as compared with their behavior a year earlier.

Theoretical writers also suggest the necessity of a school experience which is not characterized by excessive failure. In his discussion of the Juvenile Era, Sullivan (1953, p. 227) points out the importance of the school. He says, "This is the first developmental stage in which the limitations and pecularities of the home as a socializing influence begin to be open to remedy." The importance of a successful school experience is also discussed by Erikson. The stage of Industry versus Inferiority is the elementary school years. Erikson (1950, p. 227) says the child's " . . . danger, at this stage, lies in a sense of inadequacy and inferiority. If he despairs of his tools and skills or his status among his tool partners, his ego boundaries suffer, and he abandons hope for the ability to identify early with others who apply themselves to the same general section of the tool world. . . . Many a child's development is disrupted when family life may not have prepared him for school life, or when

47

school life may fail to sustain the promises of the earlier stages."

23. There have been a number of pre-school enrichment programs which have been quite successful in raising intelligence level and other cognitive as well as motivational aspects of children's development. Although the follow-up of these children into the elementary school is still in progress in most cases, data after the preschool year give reason to believe that the children will be able to show adequate elementary school performance. For reports of such preschool and kindergarten projects, see Gray and Klaus (1963), Smilansky (1964), Hess (1964c), Baltimore Report in Research Council of Great Cities Program for School Improvement (1964), and Brazziel and Terrell (1962).

24. For analyses of the elements which should be included in enrichment programs see: Hunt (1964); Smilansky (1961, 1964); Montessori (1959, 1964); Deutsch (1964b) and Ausubel (1963).

Section 4

25. See Note 22. In addition, the work of Gottlieb (1964) and S. Bloom (1960) is relevant.

26. For documentation of the cumulative deficits, see: Deutsch (1964a), Krugman (1961), Ausubel (1963), Osborne (1960), S. Bloom (1964), U. S. Office of Education (1963), Findley (1964), and Loban (1964).

27. See LeShan (1952), Mischel (1961), Rosen (1956), Rosen and D'Andrade (1959), Frankenstein (1963), Haggard (1954), Ausubel (1963), Hunt (1964) and Battle (1954).

28. See Passow (1963, p. 237) and Gottlieb (1964) regarding teachers' perceptions of slum schools. Becker (1951) and Winget (1952) have documented teacher turnover which ad-

versely affects low-income schools. See, also, Davis (1964). For examples of programs of teacher training aimed at "holding" teachers in inner-city schools see Haubrich (1963), Cleveland Report in Research Council of Great Cities Program for School Improvement (1964), and Marburger (1963b).

29.   See B. S. Bloom (1964a), especially Chapter 4, Deutsch (1964c) and Niemeyer (1964).

30.   See note 22, Ausubel (1963), and White (1959, 1963) who reviews the literature and discusses ego development and the idea of competence motivation.

31.   For examples of promising programs at the elementary-school level see Philadelphia and Detroit Reports in Research Council of the Great Cities Program for School Improvement (1964); S. Bloom (1964); Shepard (1963); Hess (1964b); Findley (1964) and U. S. Office of Education (1964).

32.   The use of tests for diagnostic purposes has been discussed and illustrated by Anastasi (1961); Larson and Olson (1963); Kirk and McCarthy (1961); Smilansky (1964); and S. Bloom (1964). Broader considerations in the use of tests with deprived children are discussed by Deutsch, Fishman et al. (1964) and Lennon (1964).

33.   The importance of a nongraded primary school is discussed by Goodlad and Anderson (1963). The work of Gagne and Paradise (1961) and Gagne et al. (1962) illustrate the sequential approach to teaching and the use of task analysis. Bruner (1964) discusses the planning of instruction. Ausubel (1963) also suggests sequential, structured instruction for the deprived child.

34.   See Shepard (1963); Marburger (1963a) New York and Los Angeles Reports in Research Council of Great Cities Program for School Improvement

(1964) as examples of such programs and U. S. Office of Education (1964).

35.   Sexton (1959) reports a very high rate of pupil turnover in schools in low-income districts. An unpublished study at the Howland School in Chicago showed that a large number of families tended to move within a relatively small area but out of school lines.

36.   For some pilot programs at the later elementary and junior high school years, see Krugman (1961), Philadelphia and Pittsburgh Reports in Research Council of Great Cities Program for School Improvement (1964); Koontz (1963), Landers (1963), S. Bloom (1964) and Marburger (1963a).

Section 5

37.   For a comprehensive summary of the literature on ego development in the Negro ghetto child, see Ausubel and Ausubel (1963). See, also, Douglass (1960), and Pettigrew (1964).

38.   Recent actions of the U. S. Supreme Court and other federal benches have been directed at eliminating prejudicial practices which have become institutionalized in law or custom on the grounds that these practices are unconstitutional and detrimental to development. See Brown et al. vs. Board of Education of Topeka, et al., decided May 17, 1954 in which the Court said: "To separate them (Negro children) from others of similar age and qualifications solely because of their race generates a feeling of inferiority as to their status in the community that may affect their hearts and minds in a way unlikely ever to be undone."

See also Hess (1964a).

39.   See Gottlieb (1964), Haubrich (1963), Kornberg (1963), Abrahamson (1952), and Havighurst and Neugarten (1962, chapter 9).

40.   Research and theory support the idea that ef-
       fective attitude change occurs when people
       participate in common activities and have di-
       rect contact. See Krathwohl, Bloom and Masia
       (1964) for a theoretical treatment. See Mor-
       ton Deutsch (1952) and Wilner et al. (1955)
       for studies of attitude change in interra-
       cial housing projects. See, also, Gottlieb
       and Houten (1964).

41.   As we have noted extensively, the cognitive
       and motivational patterns of these children
       require a curriculum which is adapted to
       their needs and states of readiness. Inte-
       grating classrooms without curricular adap-
       tations will not substantially alter cogni-
       tive growth. See Katz (1964), for a review
       of the effects of desegregation on intellec-
       tual performance.

Section 6

42.   Below-grade achievement level for deprived
       youth has been well documented. See Osborne
       (1960) and Goldberg (1963). See Siller (1957)
       for a study of socio-economic status and con-
       ceptual thinking. Dropout statistics clear-
       ly indicate the disaffection of the children
       with school. See Schreiber (1964a) and Far-
       quhar (1964).

43.   Studies have shown that participation in
       extracurricular activities at the high-school
       level is primarily limited to middle-class
       youth. See Abrahamson (1952), Hollingshead
       (1949), and Havighurst and Neugarten (1962,
       p. 245-46).

44.   For a comprehensive summary of the guidance
       problems of these youth, see Schreiber
       (1964b), Part I.

45.   Discussions of the problems of adolescence
       and the developmental tasks of this period
       may be found in Erikson (1950, 1959), and
       Havighurst (1953). Lynn (1962) discusses

formation of sex-role identity in adolescence. The vocational development of youth is analyzed by Super, et al. (1957).

46.   See Landers (1963) on the Higher Horizons Project, and Pittsburgh Project in Research Council of Great Cities Program for School Improvement (1964) which attempted to identify "more able pupils" in the later years of elementary school.

47.   Case studies of a number of work-study programs now being operated can be found in Burchill (1962). At the college level, see Wilson and Lyons (1961).

REFERENCES

Abrahamson, S., 1952. Our status system and scholastic rewards. J. Educ. Sociol., 25, 441-450.

American Council on Education, 1964. A fact book on higher education. Washington: American Council on Education.

Anastasi, Anne, 1961. Psychological tests: uses and abuses. Teachers College Record, 62, 389-393.

Ausubel, D. P., 1963. How reversible are the cognitive and motivational effects of cultural deprivation? Implications for teaching the culturally deprived child. Paper read at conference on teaching the culturally deprived child, Buffalo, New York. March 28-30, 1963.

Ausubel, D. P. and Ausubel, Pearl, 1963. "Ego development among segregated Negro children," in Passow, A. H. (Ed.), Education in depressed areas. New York: Teachers College, Columbia University.

Battle, H. J., 1954. Application of inverted analysis in a study of the relation between values and achievement of high school pupils. Unpublished Ph.D. dissertation, Univ. of Chicago.

Becker, H. S., 1951. Role and career problems of the Chicago public school teacher. Unpublished Ph.D. dissertation, Univ. of Chicago.

Berlyne, D. E., 1963. Soviet research on intellectual processes in children. Monogr. Soc. Res. Child Develpm., 28, No. 2.

Bernstein, B., 1961. "Social class and linguistic development: a theory of social learning," in Halsey, A. H., Floud, J., and Anderson, C. A. (Eds.), Education, economy and society. Glencoe: Free Press.

Bernstein, B., 1962. Linguistic codes, hesitation phenomena and intelligence. Language and Speech, 5 (1), 31-46.

Bloom, B. S., 1964a. Stability and change in human characteristics. New York: Wiley and Sons.

Bloom, B. S., Fall, 1964b, in press. The role of the educational sciences in curriculum development. Int. J. of Educ. Sciences.

Bloom, Sophie, 1960. Acculturation and school-learning among three lower-status groups. Unpublished Master's Thesis, Univ. of Chicago.

Bloom, Sophie, 1964. Procedures and materials to use with the culturally disadvantaged reader in grades IV-VIII. Proceedings of the Annual Conference on Reading held at Univ. of Chicago, 28, in press.

Brazziel, W. F. and Terrell, Mary, 1962. An experiment in the development of readiness in a culturally disadvantaged group of first grade children. J. Negro Educ., 31, 4-7.

Breckenridge, Marian E. and Vincent, E. L., 1962. "Nutrition and growth," in Seidman, J. M. (Ed.). The Adolescent - a book of readings. New York: Holt, Rinehart and Winston, Inc.

Bruner, J. S., 1960. The process of education. Cambridge: Harvard Univ. Press.

Bruner, J. S., 1964. "Some theorems on instruction illustrated with reference to mathematics," in Yearbook of National Society for Study of Education, 63 (II). Chicago: Univ. of Chicago Press.

Buckingham, W., 1962. "The impending educational revolution," in Evans, L. H. and Arnstein, G. E., Eds.), Automation and the challenge to education: Symposium on the educational implications of automation. Washington: National Education Association.

Burchill, G. W., 1962. Work-study programs for alienated youth, a casebook. Chicago: Science Research Associates.

Callahan, R. E., 1960. An introduction to education in American society, 2nd edition. New York: Alfred Knopf.

Carroll, J. B., 1960. "Language development," in Harris, C. W. (Ed.), Encyclopedia of educational research. New York: MacMillan.

Casler, L., 1961. Maternal deprivation: a critical review of the literature. Soc. Res. Child Develpm. Monogr., 26, No. 2.

Dave, R. H., 1963. The identification and measurement of environmental process variables that are related to educational achievement. Unpublished Ph.D. dissertation, Univ. of Chicago.

Davis, A., 1944. "Socialization and the adolescent personality," in Yearbook of National Society for Study of Education, 43 (1). Chicago: Univ. of Chicago Press.

Davis, A., 1948. Social-class influences upon learning. Cambridge: Harvard Univ. Press.

Davis, A., 1964. Society, the school, and the culturally deprived student. In U. S. Office of Education, Improving English skills of culturally different youth. Washington: Government Printing Office. Document # OE-30012, Bulletin 1964, No. 5.

Deutsch, M., 1963. "The disadvantaged child and the learning process," in Passow, A. H. (Ed.), Education in depressed areas. New York: Teachers College, Columbia University, 163-180.

Deutsch, M., 1964a. The role of social class in language development and cognition. New York: Institute for Developmental Studies, mimeo.

Deutsch, M., 1964b. Facilitating development in the pre-school child: social and psychological perspectives. Merrill-Palmer Q., 10, 249-263.

Deutsch, M., 1964c. "Early social environment: its

influence on school adaptation," in Schreiber, D. (Ed.), The school dropout. Washington: National Education Association.

Deutsch, M. and Brown, B., 1964. Social influences in Negro-white intelligence differences. J. Soc. Issues, 20(2), 24-35.

Deutsch, M., Fishman, J., Kogan, L., North, R., and Whiteman, M., 1964. Guidelines for testing minority group children. J. Soc. Issues, 20(2), 129-145.

Deutsch, Morton, 1952. "Social environment and attitudinal change: a study of the effects of different types of interracial housing," in Hulett, J. E. and Stagner, K. (Eds.), Problems in social psychology: an interdisciplinary inquiry. Urbana: Univ. of Illinois.

Douglass, J. H., 1960. "The effects of minority status on children," in Committee on Studies for the Golden Anniversary White House Conference on Children and Youth, Children and Youth in the 1960's: Survey papers, 181-192.

Douvan, Elizabeth, 1956. Social status and success strivings. J. Abnorm. Soc. Psychol., 52, 219-223.

Eells, K., 1951. Intelligence and cultural differences. Chicago: Univ. of Chicago Press.

Erikson, E. H., 1950. Childhood and society. New York: W. W. Norton and Co., Inc.

Erikson, E. H., 1959. The problem of ego identity. Psychological Issues, 1, No. 1.

Evans, L. H., and Arnstein, G. E. (Eds.), 1962. Automation and the challenge to education: symposium on the educational implications of automation. Washington: National Education Association.

Farquhar, W., 1964. Motivation factors related to academic achievement. Cooperative Research Project # 846, U. S. Office of Education, Washington, D. C.

56

Findley, W. G., 1964. "Language development and dropouts," in Schreiber, D. (Ed.), The school dropout.
   Washington: National Education Association.

Frankenstein, C., 1963. "The school without parents,"
   in Dushkin, A. M. and Frankenstein, C. (Eds.),
   Studies in education, Vol. 13. Jerusalem: He-
   brew University, Magnus Press.

Gagne, R. M. and Paradise, N. E., 1961. Abilities and
   learning sets in knowledge acquisition. Psychol.
   Monogr., LXXV, Whole No. 518.

Gagne, R. M., Mayor, J., Garstens, Helen and Paradise,
   N. E., 1962. Factors in acquiring knowledge of a
   mathematical task. Psychol. Monogr., LXXVI,
   Whole No. 526.

Gardner, J., 1961. Excellence: can we be equal and
   excellent too? New York: Harper Brothers.

Goldberg, Miriam L., 1963. "Factors affecting educa-
   tional attainment in depressed urban areas," in
   Passow, A. H. (Ed.), Education in depressed areas.
   New York: Teachers College, Columbia Univ.

Goodlad, J. I. and Anderson, R. H., 1963. The nongraded elementary school. New York: Harcourt,
   Brace and World, Inc.

Goodman, P., 1964. "The universal trap," in Schreiber,
   D. (Ed.), The school dropout. Washington: National Education Association.

Gottlieb, D., 1964. Teaching and students: the views
   of Negro and white teachers. Sociol. Educ., 37,
   345-353.

Gottlieb, D. and Houten, W. T., 1964, in press. The
   social systems of Negro and white adolescents.
   Transaction.

Gray, Susan and Klaus, R. A., 1963. Interim report:
   early training project. George Peabody College
   and Murfreesboro, Tenn., City Schools, mimeo.

Guilford, J. P., 1963. "The nature of intellectual activity," in The behavioral sciences and education. Princeton: College Entrance Examination Board.

Haggard, E. A., 1954. Social status and intelligence: an experimental study of certain cultural determinants of measured intelligence. Genet. Psychol. Monogr., 49, 141-186.

Harlow, H. F., 1949. The formation of learning sets. Psychol. Rev., 56, 51-65.

Harrington, M., 1962. The other America. New York: MacMillan.

Haubrich, V. F., 1963. "Teachers for big-city schools," in Passow, A. H. (Ed.), Education in depressed areas. New York: Teachers College, Columbia Univ.

Havighurst, R. J., 1953. Human development and education. New York: Longmans, Green.

Havighurst, R. J. and Neugarten, Bernice L., 1962. Society and education. Boston: Allyn and Bacon.

Hess, R. D., 1964a. Educability and rehabilitation: the future of the welfare class. Committee on Human Development, Univ. of Chicago, ditto.

Hess, R. D., 1964b. School report: action for Boston community development. Committee on Human Development, Univ. of Chicago, mimeo.

Hess, R. D., 1964c. School report: Perry pre-school project, Ypsilanti, Michigan. Committee on Human Development, Univ. of Chicago, mimeo.

Hollingshead, A. B., 1949. Elmtown's youth. New York: Wiley.

Hunt, J. McV., 1961. Intelligence and experience. New York: Ronald Press.

Hunt, J. McV., 1964. The psychological basis for using

pre-school enrichment as an antidote for cultural deprivation. Merrill-Palmer Q., 10, 209-245.

Jensen, A. R., 1965. Social class and verbal learning, in Deutsch, M. and Pettigrew, T. (Eds.), Social class, race, and psychological development. Society for the Study of Psychological Issues (in preparation).

John, Vera P., 1963. The intellectual development of slum children: some preliminary findings. Amer. J. Orthopsychiat., 33, 813-822.

Katz, I., 1964. Review of evidence relating to effects of desegregation on the intellectual performance of Negroes. Amer. Psychologist, 19, 381-399.

Keller, Suzanne, 1963. The social world of the urban slum child: some early findings. Amer. J. Orthopsychiat., 33, 823-831.

Keys, A., Henschel, A., et al., 1950. The biology of human starvation. Minneapolis: Univ. of Minnesota Press.

Kirk, S. A., 1958. Early education of the mentally retarded. Urbana: Univ. of Illinois.

Kirk, S. A., and McCarthy, J. J., 1961. The Illinois test of psycholinguistic abilities—an approach to differential diagnosis. Amer. J. Ment. Defic., 66, 399-412.

Klineberg, O., 1935. Negro intelligence and selective migration. New York: Columbia Univ. Press.

Klugman, S. F., 1944. The effect of money incentives versus praise upon the reliability and obtained scores of the Revised Stanford-Binet test. J. Gen. Psychol., 30, 255-267.

Koontz, J. D., 1963. "The Washington, D.C. program," in U. S. Office of Education, Programs for the educationally disadvantaged. Washington: Government Printing Office.

59

Kornberg, L., 1963. "Meaningful teachers for alienated
children," in Passow, A. H. (Ed.), Education for
depressed areas. New York: Teachers College,
Columbia Univ.

Krathwohl, D. R., Bloom, B. S., and Masia, B. B., 1964.
Taxonomy of educational objectives, Handbook II:
Affective domain. New York: David McKay.

Krugman, M., 1961. The culturally deprived child in
school. N.E.A.J., 50, 20-22.

Landers, J., 1963. "The higher horizons program in
New York City," in U. S. Office of Education,
Programs for the educationally disadvantaged.
Washington: Government Printing Office.

Larson, R. and Olson, J. L., 1963. A method of identifying culturally deprived kindergarten children.
Except. Children, 30, 130-134.

Lee, E. S., 1951. Negro intelligence and selective
migration: a Philadelphia test of the Klineberg
hypothesis. Amer. Sociol. Rev., 16, 227-233.

Lennon, R. T., 1964. Testing and the culturally disadvantaged child. New York: Harcourt, Brace and
World, Inc., Test Department.

LeShan, L. L., 1952. Time orientation and social class.
J. Abnorm. Soc. Psychol., 47, 589-592.

Lewis, O., 1959. Five families. New York: Basic
Books.

Loban, W., 1964. Language ability in the elementary
school: implications of findings pertaining to
the culturally disadvantaged, in U. S. Office of
Education, Improving English skills of culturally
different youth. Washington: Government Printing Office. Document # OE-30012, Bulletin, 1964,
No. 5.

Lott, A. J., and Lott, Bernice, 1963. Negro and white
youth. New York: Holt, Rinehart and Winston.

Luria, A. R., 1960. The role of speech in the regula-
tion of normal and abnormal behavior. U. S. Dept.
of Health, Education and Welfare, Russian Scientific Translation Program, Bethesda, Maryland.

Lynn, D. B., 1962. Sex-role and parental identification. Child Develpm., 33, 555-565.

Marburger, C., 1963a. "Working toward more effective
education," in U. S. Office of Education, Programs for the educationally disadvantaged. Washington: Government Printing Office.

Marburger, C., 1963b. "Considerations for educational
planning," in Passow, A. H. (Ed.), Education in
depressed areas. New York: Teachers College,
Columbia Univ.

Maslow, A. H., 1954. Motivation and personality. New
York: Harper and Row.

Miles, M. B., 1964. Innovation in education. New
York: Bureau of Publications, Teachers College,
Columbia University.

Milner, Esther, 1951. A study of the relationship between reading readiness in grade one school children and patterns of parent-child interactions.
Child Develpm., 22, 95-112.

Mischel, W., 1961. Preference for delayed reinforcement and social responsibility. J. Abnorm. Soc.
Psychol., 62, 1-7.

Montessori, Maria, 1964. The Montessori method. New
York: Schochen Books.

National Society for Study of Education, 1961. Social
forces influencing American education. Yearbook,
Volume 60, part 2. Chicago: Univ. of Chicago
Press.

Niemeyer, J. H., 1964. "Home-school interaction in relation to learning in the elementary school," in
Schreiber, D. (Ed.), The school dropout. Washington: National Education Association.

Osborne, R. T., 1960. Racial differences in mental growth and school achievement; a longitudinal study. Psychol. Rep., 7, 233-239.

Passow, A. H. (Ed.), 1963. Education in depressed areas. New York: Teachers College, Columbia Univ.

Pettigrew, T. F., 1964. A profile of the Negro American. New York: Van Nostrand.

Prescott, D., 1958. Factors that influence learning. Pittsburgh: Univ. of Pittsburgh.

Research Council of Great Cities Program for School Improvement, 1964. Promising practices from the projects for the culturally deprived. Chicago.

Riessman, F., 1962. The culturally deprived child. New York: Harper and Row.

Robbins, C. B., 1963. Higher education report. London: Her Majesty's Stationery Office.

Rosen, B. C., 1956. The achievement syndrome: a psychocultural dimension of social stratification. Amer. Sociol. Rev., 21, 203-211.

Rosen, B. C. and D'Andrade, R., 1959. The psycho-social origins of achievement motivation. Sociometry, 22, 185-218.

Schorr, A. L., 1964. The non-culture of poverty. Amer. J. Orthopsychiat., 34, 220-221.

Schreiber, D. (Ed.), 1964a. The school dropout. Washington: National Education Association.

Schreiber, D. (Ed.), 1964b. Guidance and the school dropout. Washington: National Education Association.

Sexton, Patricia C., 1959. Social class and pupil turnover rates. J. Educ. Sociol., 33, 131-134.

Shepard, S., 1963. "A program to raise the standard of school achievement," in U. S. Office of Education, Programs for the educationally disadvantaged. Washington: Government Printing Office.

Siller, J., 1957. Socio-economic status and conceptual thinking. J. Abnorm. Soc. Psychol., 55, 365-371.

Smilansky, Sarah, 1961. "Evaluation of early education," in UNESCO, Educational studies and documents, No. 42, 8-17.

Smilansky, Sarah, 1964. Progress report on a program to demonstrate ways of using a year of kindergarten to promote cognitive abilities, impart basic information and modify attitudes which are essential for scholastic success of culturally deprived children in their first two years of school. Jerusalem, Israel: Henrietta Szold Institute.

Snow, C. P., 1959. The two cultures and the scientific revolution. New York: Cambridge Univ.

Sullivan, H. S., 1953. The interpersonal theory of psychiatry. New York: W. W. Norton and Co., Inc.

Super, D., Crites, J., Hummel, R., Moser, Helen, Overstreet, Phoebe, and Warnath, C., 1957. "The process of vocational development," in Vocational Development: A framework of research. New York: Bureau of Publications, Teachers College, Columbia Univ.

Thelen, H. A., 1960. Education and the human quest. New York: Harper.

Tyler, R., 1963. "Social change and college admissions," in The behavioral sciences and education. Princeton: College Entrance Examination Board.

UNESCO, 1955. World Survey of Education.

UNESCO, 1958. World Survey of Education II: Primary Education.

U. S. Office of Education, 1959. Status of education in the U. S., No. 1. Washington: Government Printing Office.

U. S. Office of Education, 1963. Programs for the educationally disadvantaged. Washington: Government
Printing Office, Doc. No. FS 5.235:35044.

U. S. Office of Education, 1964. Improving English
skills of culturally different youth, Bulletin
No. 5. Washington: Government Printing Office,
Doc. No. OE-30012.

Vigotsky, L. S., 1962. Thought and language. New
York: Wiley.

Watson, G. (Ed.), 1963. No room at the bottom: Automation and the reluctant learner. Washington:
National Education Association.

Weaver, S. J., 1963. Interim report: psycholinguistic abilities of culturally deprived children.
George Peabody College for Teachers, mimeo.

White, R. W., 1959. Motivation reconsidered: the concept of competence. Psychol. Rev., 66, 297-333.

White, R. W., 1963. Ego and reality in psychoanalytic
theory, a proposal regarding independent ego
energies. Psychol. Issues, 3 (3), Monograph II.

Wilner, D. M., Walkley, Rosabelle P., and Cook, S. W.,
1955. Human relations in interracial housing.
Minneapolis: Univ. of Minnesota.

Wilson, J. W., and Lyons, E. H., 1961. Work-study
college programs, appraisal and report of the
study of cooperative education. New York: Harper.

Winget, J., 1952. Teacher inter-school mobility aspirations of elementary teachers, Chicago Public
School System, 1947-48. Unpublished Ph.D. dissertation, Univ. of Chicago.

Wolf, R. M., 1964. The identification and measurement of environmental process variables related
to intelligence. Unpublished Ph.D. dissertation,
Univ. of Chicago.

Wolfbein, S. L., 1964. Employment and unemployment
in the United States. Chicago: Science Research
Associates, Inc.

Part 2

AN ANNOTATED BIBLIOGRAPHY

ON

EDUCATION AND CULTURAL DEPRIVATION

Prepared by

Susan B. Silverman
Research Assistant
Department of Education
University of Chicago

INTRODUCTION AND SUMMARY

An earlier version of this bibliography was prepared as a reference document for the Research Conference on Education and Cultural Deprivation, held at the University of Chicago, June 8-12, 1964, and sponsored by the U. S. Office of Education. Since the scope of the problems relating to education and cultural deprivation encompasses many disciplines and fields of specialization, even active researchers in the field could not be well versed in all the relevant literature. We hoped, therefore, that the bibliography would serve as a basic source of some of the critical studies relevant to the problem. The participants at the Conference made extensive use of the bibliography and urged its publication as a useful source for other workers in the field.

Since the bibliography was not originally intended for publication, some additions and revisions have been made. Its content, however, remains substantially unchanged and reflects the initial purpose of the compilation. We were primarily interested in abstracts of empirical research papers which we felt were relevant to the area and had implications for practice. We included some theoretical papers which were deemed directly relevant and some essays and reports dealing with action programs in the schools, but these have not been given thorough representation.

The bibliography is not intended as a complete summary of all the research relating to education and cultural deprivation. We have selected research most helpful to the specialist and have attempted to include the more current work available. We selected works which we believed to be sound methodologically.

It is our hope that this document will be useful to research workers who are concerned with the problems of education and cultural deprivation. It is also hoped that teachers and administrators who are working with deprived children will find this material valuable.

67

We have tried to follow a fairly uniform
pattern of abstracting. Insofar as possible for
each reference we have indicated:

1. the major question, problem, or hypotheses

2. the method, sampling, and design

3. the major findings and conclusions

Citation form and abbreviations were patterned
after the Publication Manual of the American
Psychological Association.

Each reference has been categorized to
facilitate use of the bibliography. These
categories are indicated by the letters A through
G in the upper right-hand corner of each abstract.
The first letter indicates what we believe to be
the primary focus of the reference. The
categories are not completely independent. The
classifications follow:

A. Home environment and social class

B. Language

C. Cognition and learning

D. Intelligence and aptitudes

E. Personality and motivation

F. School achievement

G. School programs and personnel

To provide the reader with a brief overview of
the research contained in this bibliography, the
highlights of the research findings in each cate-
gory are described.

HOME ENVIRONMENT AND SOCIAL CLASS

The home environment has been studied as a means of understanding the factors which influence the development of children. Studies repeatedly show that the home is the single most important influence on the intellectual and emotional development of children, particularly in the preschool years.

The ways in which parents spend time with their children at meals, in play, and at other times during the day have been found to be central factors in developing skills which prepare children for school. The objects in the home, the amount of parental interest in learning, and the amount of practice and encouragement the child is given in conversation and general learning have been found to be significant influences on language and cognitive development, development of interest in learning, attention span, and motivation of the child.

Most disadvantaged children (with the possible exception of those in rural areas) spend less time in direct interaction with their parents than middle-class children do. In addition, the parents in deprived homes usually do not have the skills or the language to effectively use the time they spend with their children to foster the language and cognitive development which will help the children in school. There is much crowding and noise and children do not have an opportunity to receive corrective feedback when they begin speaking. Toys and other objects which help develop concepts are not readily available or used effectively in promoting learning.

Although parents of disadvantaged children are increasingly becoming interested in seeing their children succeed in school, they do not have the same intellectual and material resources that middle-class parents have to enable them to adequately prepare their children for the school experience. Children from deprived homes, then, come to school with a set of preschool experiences which are different from those of children from middle-class homes, and the expectations of the school do not take into consideration these differences in preschool experiences.

LANGUAGE

Research has documented the status of culturally deprived children in language development with regard to prerequisite skills, speech development, extent of vocabulary, and grammatical usage.

Adequate auditory and visual discrimination are necessary for successful speech development and for learning to read. Children from lower-class homes have been found to be weak in auditory discrimination and visual discrimination at the beginning of school. The range of oral vocabulary possessed by lower- and middle-class pupils has also been found to differ. In particular, lower-class children lack abstract language--words for categories, class names, and non-concrete ideas.

To learn words children must try them out in new situations and receive correction and extension of their vocabulary and ideas. The language deficiencies of deprived children are probably due to the ways in which language is used in the home and to the amount of practice children have in using language in the home.

The middle-class family is more likely to make use of language in an elaborated way: this includes using language to extend ideas, feelings, and individual interpretations. Language is usually accurate grammatically and allows for many ways of expressing oneself. Spoken language is the most important means of communication in the middle-class family, and children are encouraged to speak and are corrected and reinforced in their language learning.

In the deprived home, language usage is more limited. Much communication is through gestures and other non-verbal means. When language is used, it is likely to be terse and not necessarily

grammatically correct. In any case, it is likely to
be restricted, in the number of grammatical forms
which are utilized. Thus, the deprived child enters
school inadequately prepared for the typical language tasks of the first grade. The greatest handicap seems to be a lack of familiarity with the
speech used by teachers and insufficient practice in
attending to prolonged speech sequences.

In the long run, the language which the deprived
child has learned at home is likely to be
inadequate as an aid and tool in conceptualization.
Furthermore, language serves as a means of social
distinctions which can limit opportunities for
mobility.

COGNITION AND LEARNING

Some studies of learning have shown that there
is little relationship between measured
intelligence and performance on certain learning
tasks under laboratory conditions. Particularly
under the proper reinforcement conditions,
deprived children have been shown to perform just
as adequately as others.

The cognitive development of disadvantaged
children, however, is not as adequate as that of
their middle-class peers. Weaknesses in language,
limited range of experiences, and restricted
stimulation of an intellectual nature, all produce
certain cognitive deficiencies. In particular,
culturally deprived children seem to have special
difficulty in developing concepts of an abstract
nature and in generalizing. These cognitive
deficiencies become most evident in the later
elementary and junior high school grades when the
subject matter typically requires such abilities.

INTELLIGENCE AND APTITUDES

Intelligence test scores of deprived children
have been found to be lower on the average than
those of children from more stimulating
environments. The range of scores, however,
clearly indicates that there is much overlap in

the scores of deprived and middle-class children.
The IQs of disadvantaged children have been found
to show a decrease after about age five. This
seems to be part of a cumulative-deficit
phenomenon which affects both the scholastic
achievement and intelligence test performance of
these children. Some factors which have been
found to influence intelligence test performance
of disadvantaged children are motivation, rapport,
speed, and the cultural content in the tests.

A most striking finding is that the
environment of these children causes depression
of intellectual functioning, and that the
provision of a more adequate environment through
preschool and other experiences results in
considerable increase (10 to 15 points) in IQ
and in more successful school learning. Even
short-range training in perceptual skills,
following directions, and other tasks has
produced marked increases in intelligence test
performance. Thus, levels of intellectual
functioning have been found to be quite changeable
for the culturally deprived and greatly affected
by environmental experiences. In most instances
it seems correct to assume that the measured
intelligence of deprived children does not reflect
a ceiling level of their learning ability;
however, their full learning ability will be
realized only under the proper environmental
conditions in the home and the school.

PERSONALITY AND MOTIVATION

Research on personality development in deprived
children has not been very extensive. The available evidence, however, does seem to indicate that
the ego development of the deprived child is more
likely to be characterized by lack of self-confidence
and negative self-image than that of the middle-class
child. This is particularly true for the Negro deprived child who suffers the additional handicap of
caste-like status and prejudice. In the case of
males, inadequate sex-role identification seems
fairly common. In addition, research on failure
(often experienced by these children) shows negative

72

effects on personality and subsequent achievement and aspiration.

Studies of motivation show that many deprived children and adolescents often have unrealistic aspirations. Verbalized educational and occupational goals are often incongruent with actual achievement or training being received. However, on the average, students from the lower social class do have lower occupational and educational aspirations than do upper-status students.

Patterns of future-time orientation and striving for delayed, often symbolic, gratification are much more common among middle-class students than among disadvantaged students; these patterns are seen as necessary for successful academic performance. The motivational patterns of deprived children, particularly present-time orientation and reliance on immediate, often material, rewards are adaptive to their life circumstances, though not facilitative in school. The research on motivation suggests the need for developing school programs adapted to the motivational patterns of these youngsters or for developing methods which will alter these motivational and reward systems.

SCHOOL ACHIEVEMENT

The school achievement of disadvantaged children is characterized by a cumulative-deficit phenomenon. The children begin school with certain inadequacies in language development, perceptual skills, attentional skills, and motivation. Under the usual school curriculum, the achievement pattern of deprived children is such that they fall increasingly behind their non-deprived peers in school subjects. On the average, by eighth grade these children are about three years behind grade norms in reading and arithmetic as well as in other subjects. These effects are most marked in deprived children of average and low ability. One of the consequences of this cumulative deficit is that dropping out of school is much more frequent and this in turn leads to less mobility and opportunity in the occupational sphere.

The fact that the achievement deficit of these children is cumulative and increases over time seems to reflect some basic weaknesses in both curriculum and school practices for these children. It would appear from the research that it is easier to overcome these deficits in the earlier years of school than later.

SCHOOL PROGRAMS AND PERSONNEL

A number of experimental school programs for deprived children at preschool and later school levels have been initiated recently. Results of many of these programs are encouraging and indicate that curricula can be developed which can overcome many of the deficits which deprived children have. Preschool projects which emphasized development of attentional skills, language usage, concept formation, development of future-time orientation, and other readiness skills have shown promising results. Marked increases in intelligence test scores have been clearly demonstrated in these preschool programs. It seems very likely that youngsters who have had such preschool experiences will be much more ready for the usual elementary school program, although reports of performance in elementary schools of children who have been through pre-school programs are still not available because these projects are so recent.

Projects during elementary school and junior high school have also been initiated and results reported. As in the case of the preschool programs, the performance of these children improved when the curricula and materials were adapted to the children's states of readiness and provided the skills and experiences they lacked. As would be expected in light of the cumulative-deficit phenomenon, more effort and expenditure is required to help children as they become older. However, even at the junior high school level some

success has been reported in raising achievement
and aspiration levels of selected children from
low-status homes.

Research on attitudes of teachers toward
disadvantaged children generally shows more
negative evaluations of these children than of
middle-class children. Since difficulties are
often encountered in teaching deprived children,
many teachers attempt to transfer from "difficult"
schools and often blame parents and children for
classroom difficulties. The attribution of blame
and lack of rewards received by these children in
school, in addition to the many other handicaps
these children have, further interferes with
successful learning and teaching. In experimental
programs which provided teachers with curricula
more suited to these children, successful
teaching developed more positive attitudes
regarding the children and resulted in less
teacher turnover.

Abrahamson, S., 1952.
Our status system and scholastic rewards.
J. educ. Sociol., 25, 441-450.

This study investigated the relationship between
social-class level and the scholastic rewards
received by students in junior high school.

Students in seventh, eighth, and ninth grades in
two urban, two suburban, and two rural communities
were studied (N=705). Students completed questionnaires on participation in extracurricular activities, prizes received and background information;
grades were also obtained.

The social-class distribution of the school was
used as a basis for establishing the proportion of
rewards expected for each class group assuming no
class bias in distributing rewards. Findings
showed that:
1. Middle-class students received a dispropor-
   tionate share of the high grades,
2. Middle-class students occupied most class
   and school offices,
3. Extracurricular activities were participated
   in primarily by middle-class students.

Although the author did not consider the intelligence test scores of the students, he concluded that
within the schools, more scholastic rewards go to
students in the higher social classes.

Ausubel, D. P., 1963.
How reversible are the cognitive and motivational
effects of cultural deprivation? Implications
for teaching the culturally deprived child.
Paper read at a conference on the teaching of the
culturally deprived child, Buffalo, N.Y.
March 28-30.

The author examines the problem of reversibility
of the effects of cultural deprivation on verbal
and abstract intelligence and on the development of
intrinsic and extrinsic motivations for academic
achievement.

He suggests that the "critical periods" hypothesis based on studies of infrahuman species is
difficult to apply to human cognitive growth. This
hypothesis holds that some permanent retardation is
inevitable if an organism is deprived of necessary
stimulation during the period when it is maximally
susceptible to such stimulation. In humans,
particularly after the first year, rate of
maturation is relatively slow and further optimal
periods for intellectual growth have not been
demonstrated. Rather, older children and adults
seem to have definite advantage over young children
in learning new material. The possible disadvantage of postponing learnings "inheres rather
in loss of precious years of opportunity when
reasonably economical learning could have occurred
if attempted, but did not....The individual, in
comparison to equally endowed peers, incurs a
learning deficit which limits his current and
future rate of intellectual development."

The author suggests that possible irrevers-
ibility in cognitive development may result from
the "cumulative nature of intellectual deficit."
A child who has a deficit in growth is less able
to profit developmentally from new levels of
environmental stimulation. Furthermore,
intellectual development becomes increasingly
differentiated with age, and differentiation is
based on the ability to profit from new
experiences which are increasingly specialized
and complex.

He suggests that present intelligence tests
do measure "functional or operating capacity at a
given point of development" rather than innate
potential and are fair in this respect. They are
unfair to the culturally deprived in that these
children have fewer test-taking skills, are less
responsive to speed pressure, less highly
motivated, and less familiar with specific
vocabulary. However, even when these errors are
eliminated, social class differences in
intelligence still remain.

Because of language retardation in the culturally deprived, which has been documented by Deutsch, these children experience most difficulty in transition from concrete to abstract mode of thought, a transition which is necessary in the junior high school years.

Implications for education:
1. Prevention: preschool enrichment emphasizing perceptual discrimination and language development.
2. Amelioration: (a) use of more concrete-empirical props in teaching to facilitate transfer to an abstract level of cognitive functioning, (b) revision of language arts teaching to emphasize mastery in principal syntactical forms in written and oral language, rather than emphasis on grammatical forms.
3. Any teaching strategy for these children should consider: (a) state of readiness, (b) mastery of all on-going learning before new tasks are introduced, (c) use of structured learning materials optimally organized to facilitate efficient sequential learning.
4. Intrinsic motivation for learning may be most effectively developed by focusing on the cognitive, relying on motivation developed retroactively from achievement. In the long run, the development of intrinsic motivation based on successful learning may be more lasting than trying to motivate children through the use of extrinsic rewards and incentives.

E,A

Ausubel, D. P. and Ausubel, Pearl, 1963.
Ego development among segregated Negro children.
In A. H. Passow (Ed.), Education in depressed areas, New York: Teachers College, Columbia University, Pp. 109-141.

"Ego development refers to the orderly series of changes in an individual's self-concept, self-attitudes, motives, aspirations, sources of self-

esteem, and key personality traits affecting the
realization of his aspirations as he advances in a
particular cultural setting."

Summary and conclusions based on review of the
literature: "The ego development of segregated
Negro children in the U.S. manifests various
distinctive properties, both because Negroes
generally occupy the lowest stratum of the lower-
class subculture, and because they possess an
inferior caste status in American society. Their
inferior caste position is marked by an unstable
and matriarchal type of family structure, by
restricted opportunities for acquiring educational,
vocational, and social status, by varying degrees
of segregation from the dominant white majority,
and by a culturally fixed devaluation of their
dignity as human beings. The consequences of this
regrettable state of affairs for Negro children's
self-esteem and self-confidence, for their
educational and vocational aspirations, and for
their character structure, interpersonal relations,
and personality adjustment, constitute the
characteristic features of their ego development.

"Beginning in the pre-school period, the Negro
child gradually learns to appreciate the negative
implications of dark skin color for social status
and personal worth. Hence he resists
identifying with his own racial group and shows
definite preference for white dolls and playmates.
This reluctance to acknowledge his racial
membership not only results in ego deflation, but
also makes it difficult to identify with his
parents and to obtain from such identification the
derived status that universally constitutes the
principal basis for self-esteem during childhood.
Much of the derived status that white children
obtain from their parents is made available to the
Negro child by virtue of his membership in an
unsupervised peer group, which accordingly performs
many of the socializing functions of the white-
middle-class home. This is especially true for the
Negro boy who often has no adult male with whom to
identify in the frequently fatherless Negro family,

79

and who finds maleness deprecated in his matriarchal and authoritarian home. Early experience in fending for himself results in precocious social maturity, independence, and emancipation from the home.

"During pre-adolescence and adolescence, segregated Negro children characteristically develop low aspirations for academic and vocational achievement. These low aspirations reflect existing social class and ethnic values, the absence of suitable emulatory modes, marked educational retardation, restricted vocational opportunities, lack of parental and peer group support, and the cultural impoverishment of the Negro home. Because of loyalty to parents and rejection by the dominant white group, Negro adolescents develop ambivalent feelings toward middle-class achievement values and the personality traits necessary for their implementation. Girls tend to develop a more mature ego structure than boys probably because of their favored position in the home."

E,A

Battle, Esther S. and Rotter, J. B., 1963. Children's feeling of personal control as related to social class and ethnic group. J. Pers., 31, 482-490.

A personality variable, external versus internal control, was studied in relation to children's social status and race. People with internal control accept personal responsibility for what happens to them, while people with external control attribute responsibility outside themselves. Eighty Negro and white school children (grades 6 and 8) were studied. A cartoon test and questionnaire were administered.

The main findings included:
1. A relationship between control and social class existed. Middle-class children were more internally controlled than lower-class children.

80

2. Lower-class Negroes were more externally controlled than middle-class Negroes and whites.
3. Sex differences in control were not found.

G

Baynham, D., 1963.
The great cities project.
Nat. Educ. Ass. J., 52 (4), 17-20.

The author of this article reviewed programs in the Great Cities Project. He noted five common factors:
1. Culturally deprived students are recognized as usually poor in communication skills and this inability causes failure in other subjects.
2. The schools involved demonstrate a willingness to experiment with a broad range of teaching materials such as film strips, records, and television, and with administrative approaches such as team teaching and flexible programming.
3. The schools involved demonstrate strenuous efforts to search out and use community help such as various public health and welfare services or private philanthropic organizations and business and industry.
4. Teachers involved in the programs are receiving training in teaching skills and attitudes, and their involvement in the projects is producing enthusiasm and devotion.
5. The schools involved are using lay personnel to interpret the efforts of the schools to the community and to obtain community reactions.

B,A

Bernstein, B., 1961.
Social class and linguistic development: a theory of social learning.
In A. H. Halsey, J. Floud, and C. A. Anderson (Eds.), Education, economy and society. Glencoe: The Free Press, Pp. 288-314.

The author discusses the centrality of language in socialization and the ways in which language depends on social structure and relationships. He postulates linguistic differences associated with social-class membership.

He proposes two linguistic codes: formal (later termed elaborated) and public (later termed restricted). Most middle-class children learn both formal and public codes. Most working-class children are restricted to the use of a public code. Formal code is grammatically more complex, allows for elaboration of meaning and subjective feelings, and "points to the possibilities inherent in a complex conceptual hierarchy for the organizing of experience." Public language is simple grammatically and does not allow precise statement of ideas or emotions. It is a language in which much meaning is assumed or implicit.

The implications of these linguistics differences for the cognitive, social, and affective development of children are discussed. The effects of these codes on performance in school are also examined.

B,A,C

Bernstein, B., 1962.
Linguistic codes, hesitation phenomena and intelligence.
Language and Speech, 5 (1), 31-46.

Two linguistic codes have been proposed, elaborated and restricted. These codes are regarded as functions of different social structures. They are considered to entail qualitatively different verbal planning orientations which control different modes of self-regulation and levels of cognitive behaviour. Social class differences in the use of these codes were postulated and the hesitation phenomena associated with them pre-dicted.

Speech samples were obtained and the hesitation phenomena analysed from a discussion situation in-volving small groups of middle-class and working-class subjects with varying I.Q. profiles.

Major results

(1) Overall social class differences were found. The working-class subjects used a longer mean phrase length, spent less time pausing and used a shorter word length.
(2) Holding non-verbal intelligence constant, social class differences were found in the same direction.
(3) Holding verbal and non-verbal intelligence constant, social class differences were again found in the same direction, but not for word length.
(4) Within the middle-class group, the sub-group with superior verbal intelligence used a longer mean phrase length, a faster rate of articulation and a longer word length.
(5) Within the working-class group, the sub-group with the average I.Q. profile spent less time pausing.

The major predictions were confirmed. The results were considered supporting evidence for the two codes and the different verbal planning orientations which are entailed.

(Author's Summary)

F,A,E

Bledsoe, J. C., 1959.
An investigation of six correlates of student withdrawal from high school.
J. educ. Res., 53, 3-6.

Six factors were investigated in relation to school dropouts: (1) sex, (2) size of class in first through eighth grades, (3) stability of elementary enrollment, (4) parent occupation, (5) level of parent education, and (6) level of reading comprehension.

Case histories of 247 students in a Georgia town of 20,000 were examined. These students had dropped out of school in eighth, ninth, or tenth grades.

The findings indicated that more boys than girls dropped out of school. The relation between size

of class and dropping out was not consistent.
Stable groups had fewer dropouts; that is, 3.8
times as many students who shifted enrollment in
grade school dropped out as did those who had
stable enrollment. There were significantly more
dropouts among students whose parents were unskilled laborers or unemployed as compared with
students whose parents were in professional,
managerial, agricultural, or clerical jobs.
Also, as might be expected, there was a high incidence of dropping out among children with parents of low educational level. Reading comprehension scores for students who dropped out of
the ninth and tenth grades averaged 7.9 compared
with 8.9 for those students remaining in the
ninth grade.

A,D,F,C,E

Bloom, B. S., 1964.
Stability and change in human characteristics.
New York: Wiley and Sons.

This book examines and interprets data from
about 1,000 longitudinal studies on the shaping
of human characteristics from infancy to adult-
hood. It includes data on physical characteristics, intelligence, achievement data, interests,
attitudes, and personality. The research findings are related to three propositions:

1. The relation between parallel measurements
   over time is a function of the levels of
   development represented at the different
   times.
2. Change measurements are generally unrelated to initial measurements but they are
   highly related to the relevant environmental conditions in which individuals
   have lived during the change period.
3. Variations in the environment have greatest quantitative effect on a characteristic at its most rapid period of change
   and least effect on the characteristic
   during the least rapid period of change.

In general, the findings reveal the tremendous
importance of the first few years of life for all

84

that follows. Change in many characteristics
becomes more and more difficult with increasing
age and only the most powerful environmental conditions are likely to produce significant
changes at later stages of life.

A, E

Bloom, R., Whiteman, M., and Deutsch, M., 1963.
Race and social class as separate factors related
to social environment.
Paper read at American Psychological Association
meeting, Philadelphia, September, 1963.

This study attempted to separate out the
variables of race and social class in determining
social environment. The sample consisted of 292
pairs of parents and first- and fifth-grade
children with similar proportions of Negro and
white in three social class levels. Social class
was measured by educational level and prestige
rating of the main support of the family. Data
were based on personal interviews with the children
and parents' responses to a questionnaire.
Dependent variables included housing conditions,
aspirations, mobility, family life and conditions.

Findings revealed two characteristics in which
Negroes are similar to the lower-class group: high
frequency of housing dilapidation and absence of
father from the home. In this study where race and
social class were independent, Negroes reported more
middle-class motivation than whites, that is, higher
educational and occupational aspirations for their
children. The Negro children themselves aspired to
higher occupations than the white children. Housing
of lower-class groups is more crowded, there is less
occupational mobility, and children have substandard
breakfasts more often, but these Negro-white differences are non-significant. There is a significantly greater tendency for Negro than for white
mothers to be away from their children at breakfast.
In general, however, the relationship between social
class and environmental conditions are similar in
both the white and Negro samples.

It was concluded that social class seems to be
a more potent variable than race in predicting
environmental and attitudinal factors.

A,C,E,G

Bloom, Sophie, 1960.
Acculturation and school-learning among three
lower-status groups.
Unpublished masters paper, University of Chicago.

This paper examines three diverse cultural
groups: Puerto Ricans in New York City, Negroes
in the United States, and Oriental Jews in Israel.
It includes a description of the values and
behaviors of each group and factors which influence
their acculturation.

Common elements in all three groups are
identified and a learning-theory analysis of the
role of the school in assisting students from these
cultures is presented. Although these groups are
very different in origin, they all represent
groups which can be described as culturally disadvantaged in terms of their adjustment to the
main society in which they live and their
children's adaptation to the schools.

D,F,G,B

Boger, J. H., 1952.
An experimental study of the effects of perceptual
training on group IQ scores of elementary pupils in
rural ungraded schools.
J. educ. Res., 46, 43-53.

This study provided rural white and Negro
children with stimulating visual materials involving reasoning ability of a perceptual nature to
determine whether such training would enhance performance on subsequent intelligence tests.

Experimental subjects were 25 white and 29 Negro
children in grades 1-4. Control subjects were 22
Negro and 28 white children. Each group was an
intact rural classroom under a single teacher. The
Otis Quick-Scoring Mental Ability Test and the
California Test of Mental Maturity were given to

the control and experimental groups before the
training period for the latter was begun (January),
in May of the same year after training, and the
following October. The five-month training period
was to provide practice in following directions,
noting details, perceiving spatial relationships,
detecting likeness and difference in pictorial
and geometric patterns, and developing increased
co-ordination of eye and hand movements. Practice
materials used by the experimental groups consisted of geometric designs and puzzles, jigsaw
puzzles, and wood puzzles.

The total group of rural children was below
average on the norms for the intelligence tests.
Both white and Negro experimental groups showed significant increases in total IQs and California non-
language scores after training. Both groups also
showed significant gains on Spatial Relationships
and Logical Reasoning subtests of the California
Test. On the Otis verbal, white experimental gain
was 8.2 points compared with 3.0 points gain for
the white control group. Negro experimental group
gained 6.9 points on the Otis verbal as compared
with 0.2 for the Negro control group. On the
California non-language, white experimental gain
was 14.9, control gain was 3.8; Negro experimental
gain was 15.2, control gain was 0.2. Gains were
maintained on the October testing, five months after
the training period.

It was suggested that training in visual perception may enable rural pupils to react more
effectively in situations requiring perceptual
discrimination (for example, reading, spelling,
arithmetic) and may cause an increase in intelligence test scores. "The extent of improvement as
a result of training indicates (1) that scores
from IQ tests often give an estimate of mental
ability which is an injustice to these pupils so
far as actual ability is concerned, and (2) that
perceptual training remedies some of the handicaps which influence performance of rural children
on group IQ tests. It would appear that rural
elementary school children are capable of
responding to a more challenging school program

than IQ scores derived from group intelligence
tests frequently seem to justify."

Boyd, G. F., 1952.
The levels of aspiration of white and Negro children
in a non-segregated elementary school.
J. soc. Psychol., 36, 191-196.

This study attempted to assess whether there
was a measurable difference in level of aspiration
between white and Negro children of the same intelligence level in an elementary school in Portland,
Oregon.

Twenty-five Negro and 25 white children were
matched for age, economic status, and IQ. Level
of aspiration was measured in two ways. A target
test and an arithmetic test were administered and
the level of aspiration was the discrepancy between
actual score and that expected for the next trial
by the child. A questionnaire designed to get at
verbalization regarding future hopes and plans was
also used.

The results obtained indicated that the Negro
group had the higher level of aspiration in both
the test situation and the questionnaire responses.

G,B,D

Brazziel, W. F. and Terrell, Mary, 1962.
An experiment in the development of readiness in a
culturally disadvantaged group of first-grade
children.
J. Negro Educ., 31, 4-7.

This paper reported a six-week readiness program for 26 Negro first-grade children. The
program included parent meetings once a week, 30
minutes of educational TV watched in the home, and
a readiness program to develop vocabulary, perception, word reasoning, and ability to follow
directions.

At the end of six weeks the experimental class
was at the 50th percentile on readiness as measured

by the Metropolitan Readiness Test, while the three
non-experimental classes in the same school were at
the 15th percentile. This difference was significant. IQ after seven months was 106.5, while the
general expectation for group is 90.

A, E

Bronfenbrenner, U., 1961.
The changing American child - a speculative analysis.
Merrill-Palmer Q. 7, (2), 73-84.

This is a summary of the effects on children of
the changing patterns of child rearing. Some of
the generalizations drawn from the literature
follow:

Changing American Parent (over the last 26 years)
1. Greater permissiveness and freer expression
   of affection, reasoning, guilt
2. Increased reliance on psychological
   techniques of discipline
3. A narrowing of the gap between social
   classes in patterns of child rearing.

Psychological Techniques of Discipline
4. "Love-oriented" psychological techniques are
   very powerful in bringing about desired
   behavior in child.
5. Girls are more likely to be subjected to
   "love-oriented" discipline than boys are.
   Girls are found to be more obedient, more
   cooperative, and better socialized than
   boys. Girls tend to become "oversocialized."
6. First children are more exposed to
   psychological techniques and tend to become
   more anxious and more dependent than later
   children.
7. Girls are susceptible to the detrimental
   influences of overprotection, while boys are
   susceptible to the effects of insufficient
   parental discipline and support.

Class Differences
8. Overprotection for girls is a greater danger
   in lower-class families than in middle-
   class families.

89

9. Boys are in greater danger of inadequate discipline in lower middle-class than in upper middle-class families.
10. In higher socio-economic levels, girls excel boys in responsibility and social acceptance.
11. In lower middle-class, boys excel girls in leadership, level of aspiration, and competitiveness.

Family Structure

12. Mothers primarily use love-oriented techniques of discipline (at each social level), while fathers use direct methods at lower levels and love-oriented techniques at higher social levels.
13. Fathers tend to use love-oriented techniques with girls and direct methods with boys.
14. Boys tend to be more responsible when father is the principal disciplinarian and girls are more dependable when mother is the major authority figure.
15. Boys from father-absent homes tend to be dependent. Absence of father is especially critical for male children.

Looking Forward

16. Emphasis on intellectual achievement is becoming the dominant force in redirecting aims and methods of child rearing in the U.S. In addition to producing high achievement motivation in children, some undesirable personality characteristics may accompany such training. The author suggests that children may become more aggressive, cruel, domineering, and tense as a result of achievement training.

A,B,C

Casler, L., 1961.
Maternal deprivation: a critical review of the literature.
Soc. Res. Child Develpm. Monogr., 26, No. 2.

The author summarizes the main findings from many studies on maternal deprivation, drawing on literature which represents the institutional approach, the cultural approach, animal experimentation, and neuroanatomical hypotheses. He concludes:

1. Emotional, physical, and intellectual malfunctioning is known to occur with frequency among children in many institutions.
2. Some authors have alleged that this malfunctioning is attributable to the deprivation of maternal love.
3. It is more likely, however, that deprivation of maternal love can have ill effects only after specific affective responsiveness has been achieved by the child (usually at about the age of six months). Ill effects found in children maternally deprived before this age probably have some other cause.
4. Evidence is accumulating, both on the human and animal level, that this "other cause" is perceptual deprivation--the absolute or relative absence of tactile, vestibular, and other forms of stimulation.
5. Those forms of social stimulation necessary for proper language development, etc., can be provided within an institutional setting.
6. Recent neuroanatomical findings, especially those concerning the reticular formation, help to explain why perceptual stimulation is so important for normal development.

(Author's Summary)

E

Clark, K. B. and Clark, Mamie K., 1939.
The development of consciousness of self and the emergence of racial identification in Negro preschool children.
J. soc. Psychol., 10, 591-599.

This study investigated the development of consciousness of self in Negro preschool children, particularly with regard to emergent race consciousness.

A modification of the Horowitz picture technique was used with 150 Negro children in segregated

Washington, D. C. nursery schools (75 boys and 75 girls). Three-, four- and five-year-old children were equally represented.

On the entire series of pictures more choices were made of the colored boy. Among the boys, each successive age group had more choices in favor of the colored boy. The percentage of choices of the colored boy increased from the three-year level (41.2 per cent) to the four-year level (55.4 per cent) and slightly at the five-year level (56.0 per cent). The choices of the boys show significant trends, but those of the girls do not. The author suggested that this difference may be due to the fact that the boys were making identifications of themselves, while the girls were identifying brothers, cousins, and in a few instances, a boy playmate. This study suggests that at least for Negro boys the process of racial identification begins early in the preschool years. The evidence for Negro girls is not so clear but this may have been a function of the method used.

A,D

Clarke, A. D. B. and Clarke, A. M., 1953.
How constant is the I.Q.?
Lancet, ii, 877-880.

Drawing on studies which dispel the notion that IQ is constant over long periods of time, the authors attempted to extend this finding to mental defectives.

Main experiment entailed retesting of 59 adolescent and adult subjects after an average of 27 months had elapsed since first testing with Wechsler test. All subjects were certified mental defectives at first testing.

Found that 27 patients had increased scores by 8 points or more, 17 by 10 points or more, and 7 by 15 points or more (maximum increase was 25). Other 32 patients showed small positive or negative increments.

An attempted explanation of these data led to investigation of the home environments of the patients. Criteria of adverse home conditions were formulated, including court intervention, parental attitude antagonistic to the child, home dirty and neglected, gross poverty, deficiency diseases, and others. Fifty-nine case histories were examined for evidence of adverse conditions (any 2 of list). Twenty-five cases found to fit "very bad homes," others (34) no evidence of such conditions.

Differences between IQ gains of the group from very adverse early environment (mean = + 9.7) and the remainder (mean = + 4.1) were significant at .01 level. Average age of entire population was 24 years (range 14-50), initial IQ range 35-98 with a mean of 66.2. Retest range was 49-97 with mean of 72.7.

"It is consistent with this finding to suggest that the environment which is really antagonistic towards the child retards mental development for many years. Later, however, after removal from such conditions this retardation begins to fade, and I.Q. increments occur, often at ages when mental growth is commonly assumed to have ceased."

A further validation of the hypothesis was carried out on another group of defectives--6 from adverse home conditions, 5 not. Patients had been tested 2 years earlier and were retested. Adverse group showed an increment of + 8.7 while non-adverse group showed gain of + 0.6.

"The results show clearly that intellectual retardation among such deprived people as have been studied here is not necessarily a permanent and irreversible condition."

F,D,G,A

Coleman, H. A., 1940.
The relationship of socio-economic status to the performance of junior high school students.
J. exp. Educ., 9, 61-63.

This was a survey of the relationships between socioeconomic status and intelligence, school achievement, and participation in school

activities. A national sample of 4,784 junior high
school students was studied. The Kuhlmann
Anderson I. Q., Units Scales of Attainment Battery
and Sims Socio-Economic Score Card were
administered. The students were divided into three
status groups. A fourth group was made up of
students whose families were on relief.

Some findings were:
1. Differences in median IQ scores were
   between 7 and 14 points among status groups.
2. Reading-score differences were between 5 and
   11 months on grade norms for status groups.
3. Differences in geography, history, and
   problem-solving tests consistently favored
   high-status group.
4. Intellectual hobbies and participation in
   extracurricular activities were greater for
   high group.
5. A personal inventory showed greater mal-
   adjustment in the low group, but little
   difference between the average- and high-
   status groups.
6. The group on relief was very similar on all
   measures to the low-status group.

The author concluded that the school's extracurricular program seems to be organized to fit the
upper-status group. The school needs to adapt its
curricular and extracurricular offerings to children
from different socioeconomic backgrounds.

E,F

Coleman, J. S., 1960.
The adolescent subculture and academic achievement.
Amer. J. Sociol., 65, 337-347.

This study examined the status systems in
several high schools, the effects of these status
systems on individuals within them, and the possible source of these systems.

The sample consisted of ten midwest high
schools--five in small towns, one in a working-
class suburb, one in a well-to-do suburb, and three
in cities of varying sizes. All but one, a

Catholic boy's school, were coeducational and public. Two upper middle-class private schools were also included to answer certain questions arising from the analysis of the data from the original ten schools. Data were school grade records, intelligence test results, and questionnaires on how the student would most like to be remembered in his school and what was required for entrance into the "leading crowd."

Boys chose to be remembered as an athletic star in preference to most popular or brilliant student. Girls chose leader in activities and most popular over brilliant student. In the two private schools, it was found that the boys tended to choose "brilliant student" as the way they would like to be remembered. This tendency was not evident for the girls in the private schools.

The author explained these results in terms of values of the adolescents within a particular social system. In the first ten high schools studied, prestige and status were awarded in non-academic areas. It was suggested that in high-school social systems which do not reward scholastic achievement, those students considered as "intellectuals" will not be the ones with the most ability. Instead, the most able students will seek status in other more profitable areas. Lack of status associated with scholastic achievement may be related to emphasis on inter-scholastic athletics. The author suggested that interscholastic competition in academic areas would correspondingly affect the status systems.

C,D,G

Covington, M. V., 1962.
Some effects of stimulus familiarization on discrimination.
Unpublished doctoral dissertation, University of California.

This is a study of differences in visual perceptaul ability in children entering kindergarten and the effects of training on this ability. Seventy-two children were subjects for the study.

95

They were divided into four groups, by social status and by treatment. Upper-status children had parents who both had some college training; lower-status children had parents with no training beyond high school.

On a visual discrimination test, in which children matched an abstract form to the same form in a cluster of three forms, upper-status children scored significantly higher than lower-status children. The experimental groups then viewed the standard forms on 13 consecutive school days. The forms were projected on a screen and the children were merely instructed to look at them. The control groups received the same treatment except that pictures rather than the abstract forms were projected for their viewing.

Both the upper- and lower-status experimental groups improved in their scores on the discrimination test, while the control groups showed little gain. Further, the lower-status group gain was significantly greater than the upper-status group gain. This suggests that the lower-status group profited most from familiarity with the stimulus objects. In fact, the post-test scores of the two status groups were not significantly different, suggesting that the upper-status group was near maximal performance prior to the treatment.

This study shows that differences in perceptual ability are likely to exist between children coming from varying social classes, particularly since the lower-status group in this study did not represent the extremes of low status in the society as a whole.

F,D,A

Curry, R. L., 1962.
The effect of socio-economic status on the scholastic achievement of sixth-grade children.
Brit. J. educ. Psychol., 32, 46-49.

The purpose of this study was to determine whether there were significant differences in

scholastic achievement between children of comparable intellectual ability but differing socio-
economic status (SES).

Subjects were 360 sixth-grade children from 33
elementary schools in a large city in southwestern
U. S. Three levels of intellectual ability were
determined by use of the California Test of Mental
Maturity. The California Achievement Tests were
used to measure scholastic achievement. SES was
determined by a questionnaire to parents and
divided into three levels.

In the high-intelligence group, no significant
differences were found in scholastic achievement
between the three SES levels. In the medium-
intelligence group, higher SES was significantly
related to better language achievement and total
achievement scores, but this relationship did not
hold for reading and arithmetic. In the low-
ability group, reading, language, and total
achievement varied according to SES. The over-all
finding of this study was that as intellectual
ability decreases from high to low, the effect of
social and economic conditions on scholastic
achievement increases greatly. Only arithmetic
seems to be relatively free of this influence.

The author concluded: "In this investigation
it is shown that when a child has above average
intellectual ability ⌐ as demonstrated by high
test scores ⌐ he will probably overcome the effects
of a deprived home environment. However, as the
intellectual ability decreases, the effect of deprived social and economic conditions of the home
begins to have a more serious effect on scholastic
achievement."

F,A

Dave, R. H., 1963.
The identification and measurement of environmental
process variables that are related to educational
achievement.
Unpublished doctoral dissertation, University of
Chicago.

It was hypothesized on the basis of the

97

literature that the home environment relevant to educational achievement might be studied in terms of six variables: (1) achievement press, (2) language models in the home, (3) academic guidance provided in the home, (4) stimulation provided in the home to explore various aspects of the larger environment, (5) the intellectual interests and activity in the home, and (6) the work habits emphasized in the home. Sixty mothers were interviewed and the ratings on their responses were related to the scores of their children on a battery of achievement tests taken at the end of the fourth grade of school.

The over-all index of the home environment had a correlation of + .80 with the total score on the entire achievement battery. The correlations between the home environment and parts of the achievement test are highest with the tests of word knowledge and reading and they are lowest with spelling and arithmetic computation. This suggests that the home has the greatest influence on the language development of the child and the least influence on skills taught primarily in the school.

The correlation of + .80 may be contrasted with the much lower correlation (usually less than .50) between school achievement and other indices of the home environment such as socio-economic status, education of parents, occupational status, or social class. If supported by further research, these techniques may enable the school to analyze the home environment and to determine the best strategy for the school and the home to provide the environmental conditions necessary for school achievement. This approach also makes it clear that parents with relatively low levels of education or occupational status can provide very stimulating home environments for educational achievement. It is what the parents do in the home rather than their status characteristics which are most influential on the achievement of their children.

A,E,G

Davidson, Helen H., Riessman, F., and
Meyers, Edna, 1962.
Personality characteristics attributed to the
worker.
J. soc. Psychol., 57, 155-160.

This was a study of personality characteristics
attributed to various occupational groups. It was
hypothesized that persons in higher occupational
categories would be rated more positively in personality characteristics than persons in lower
occupational groups. Asch's technique for
obtaining impressions of personality was adapted
to test the hypothesis.

Subjects were 241 undergraduate men and women
ranging in age from about 17 to 20 years. The
social class of the subjects ranged from lower to
upper. A check list of 30 personality
characteristics was used to determine students'
images or stereotypes of selected occupational
groups: factory owner, factory worker, assistant
office manager, teacher, and physician.

The occupational groups differed significantly
in 12 of the 30 characteristics. Positive
characteristics were distributed about equally
among the factory owner, assistant office manager,
teacher, and physician. The worker had the lowest
mean score for all these qualities. More negative
characteristics were attributed to factory workers
than to any of the other occupational groups.
Among the twelve characteristics having statistical
significance, only two indicated positive
evaluation of the worker. Lowest mean scores were
ascribed to the worker on the remaining ten
characteristics; these included "practical,"
"thoughtful," "serious," "polite," "confident,"
and "intelligent."

It was concluded that the subjects--many of
whom were prospective teachers, psychologists, and
social workers--had decidedly unfavorable images
of the worker. Such images were seen as destructive
to the purposes of the school system.

A,F,E

Davie, J., 1953.
Social class factors and school attendance.
Harvard educ. Rev., 23, 175-185.

This was a study of the relationship between
the position of the family in the social-class
structure and the educational pattern of its
children.

High school records of all 16- and 17-year olds
(N = 3,736) in New Haven were studied. Each family
was classified on the basis of area of residence,
and the child was classified on type of educational
institution he was attending (trade school, high
school, private secondary school, etc).

A high relationship was found between social
class and non-attendance, trade school, private
school, and early entrance into liberal arts
college. When a sample of families was interviewed
for typical views of each class about education,
it was found that finances were very important in
educational decisions for some classes. In
addition, custom (the tendency to educate children
at equal or better level than the parents), and
the purpose or value of education for each group
were the important variables in their educational
decisions.

It was concluded that "the pattern of schooling
is partially determined by the mere fact of birth
into a particular family with a particular social
class status. A considerable portion of the
individual's life as an adult is influenced in his
early years. The school appears to be per-
petuating the status of some children and is
serving as a channel of upward mobility for others.
This study and others bring into question the myth
that the United States is a classless society and
that there is equal educational opportunity for
all."

Davis, A., 1944.
Socialization and the adolescent personality.
In Yearb. nat. Soc. Stud. Educ., 43, Part 1,
Chicago: U. of Chicago Press, Pp. 198-216.

This is a theoretical paper which develops the
hypothesis that "the successful socialization of
the adolescent depends upon the degree of
adaptive, or socialized, anxiety which has been
instilled in him by his society." Socialized
anxiety leads to striving for rewards and concern
lest the rewards not be obtained.

Adolescents learn the culture of the group to
which they belong and in which they are
socialized. Compared to both lower- and higher-
status adolescents, the middle-class adolescent is
more deeply motivated to achieve. In lower-class
society, aggression is socially approved; in
middle-class society, ambition is approved.

The author suggests that, "the problem of
American public education is to learn to
motivate low-status children with socially adaptive
anxiety and to convince them of the reality of the
rewards at the end of the climb."

A,B,C,E

Deutsch, M., 1963.
The disadvantaged child and the learning process.
In A. H. Passow (Ed.), Education in depressed
areas, New York: Teachers College Columbia
University, Pp. 163-180.

"The thesis here is that the lower-class child
enters the school situation so poorly prepared to
produce what the school demands that initial
failures are almost inevitable, and the school
experience becomes negatively rather than positively reinforced...."

The main factors which affect the child's lack
of readiness for school are outlined. One such
factor is lack of variety of stimulation in the
home. This includes visual, tactile, and

101

auditory stimulation. Few objects are in the home
to help development of visual discrimination
skills. A lack of manipulatable objects reduces
tactile development.` There is much noise in the
lower-class environment, but little direct
communication and feedback. In such circumstances
children may learn skills of inattention to drown
out noise.

There is a lack of expectation of reward for
performance and most tasks are "motoric, have a
short-time span, and are more likely to be related
to concrete objects or services for people."

Data indicate that class differences in perceptual abilities and general environmental
orientation decrease with age, while language
differences tend to increase. If language is taken
as prerequisite to concept formation and problem-
solving, then this deficit has tremendous effect
at all levels of learning.

                                          G,F,E
Deutsch, M., 1964.
Early social environment: its influence on school
adaptation.
In D. Schreiber (Ed.), The school dropout.
Washington, D. C.: Nat. Educ. Ass., Pp. 89-100.

The author views the preschool program as a
means of accommodation between the school and the
child and his family. "The differences in the
interaction among the child, the school, and the
community, are determined, among other things, by
social attitudes toward education, stability of
community, social class and ethnic membership of
family, and sex of child."

Differences in preparation for school are evident between middle-class and lower-class
preschool children: the middle-class child is
more likely to be better prepared. The author
states that "for the lower-class child, school
failure may result in less personal upset or dis-
turbance ⌐than for the middle-class child ⌐ but
may be more final, both in terms of recovery of

102

adequate functioning in school and in terms of occupational choices."

The author states that "children who have had a preschool and kindergarten experience are more likely to cope appropriately with the kinds of things the school demands intellectually than are children who have not had this experience."

Preliminary data indicated that preschool, kindergarten, or day-care experience, or a combination of these, was associated with higher group intelligence test scores; the scores are higher in the first grade, and the differential tends to be accentuated in a fifth-grade population; the differential holds even when social class is controlled.

B,C,A

Deutsch, M., 1964.
The role of social class in language development and cognition.
Institute for Developmental Studies, New York.
Mimeo.

This study examined language and cognitive variables on a sample of 292 white and Negro children in first and fifth grades. Relationships between socio-economic status (SES), race, grade, and language variables were studied.

Significant correlations with race were found less frequently for the first-graders than for the fifth-graders. The number of significant comparisons on SES for each grade level was constant. The functions underlying measures for which race is associated with poor performance are found in the areas of abstraction, verbalization, and experientially dependent enumeration. Further, the deficiency based on class and race is on the measures which reflect abstract and categorical use of language, as opposed to denotative and labeling usage.

The author concludes that the data support the cumulative deficit hypothesis which he has

advanced. Although there are differences by SES
and race at the first-grade level, they became
more marked, as the child goes through the early
years of school. Taking into account the
initial inadequacies of these children at school
entrance, the decline in their performance relative to others brings into question the adequacy
of the educational institution.

D,A

Deutsch, M. and Brown, B., 1964.
Social influences in Negro-white intelligence
differences.
J. soc. Issues, 20 (2), 24-35.

This was an investigation of some factors which
influence the development of intellective functioning in children. The study was based on 543 urban
children stratified by race, social class, and grade
level (first and fifth). Lorge-Thorndike, Level I,
Primary Battery was administered to first-graders;
Level 3 of same test was administered to fifth-
graders.

Mean IQ was significantly higher for white than
for Negro groups: Negro children at each socio-
economic (SES) level score lower than white children
at same level and Negro-white differences increase
at each higher SES level. (SES I: Negro = 91,
white = 97; SES II: Negro = 95, white = 106; SES
III: Negro = 103, white = 115). Further investigation showed a significantly lower score for children
in father-absent homes as compared to children in
intact families, using SES I and SES II only. This
finding is more marked at the fifth-grade level than
at the first-grade level. The result suggests either
a cumulative effect of father-absence or elements in
the test at grade 5 which directly relate to father's
role in the family (especially, "variety of activities in which family participates"). Effects of
preschool experience were also examined for SES I and
SES II. At the fifth-grade level, the IQs of children who had attended preschool were significantly
higher than those of children who had not. At first
grade the trend was evident, but not statistically
significant.

It was concluded that as social-class level increases, the influence of race becomes increasingly
manifest. These findings support the author's cumulative deficit hypothesis: that deprivational influences have greater effect on later developmental
stages than on earlier ones.

D

Deutsch, M., Fishman, J., Kogan, L., North, R., and
Whiteman, M., 1964.
Guidelines for testing minority group children.
J. soc. Issues, 20 (2), 129-145.

This is a summary of relevant considerations
for professionals who use tests with minority-
group children. Reliability and validity are
discussed, with particular reference to effects
of using atypical populations--dissimilar to those
on which the test was standardized. Suggestions
on interpretation of test results and test
administration are outlined.

The use of tests as evaluative, prognostic, and
diagnostic instruments which assist in assessing
the goals of the educative process for a given
child is seen as central.

B,D,A

Deutsch, M., Maliver, Alma, Brown, B., and
Cherry, Estelle, 1964.
Communication of information in the elementary
school classroom.
U. S. Office of Education, Cooperative Research
Project No. 908.

This is a study of the language used by 62 first-
grade children and 105 fifth-grade children who
varied in social-class status and race. "The major
findings of the Expressive and Receptive Language
Studies may be summarized as follows:
1. While fifth grade children were found to be
more productive on every language measure than first
graders were, in general the proportion of any language score to the total output of speech was the
same at both grade levels.
2. Three relatively discrete factors of inter-
related language and/or demographic variables were

105

obtained for each of the two age groups studied.
These clusters indicated that: (a) Many of the traditional language measures yielded overlapping results owing to their high degree of dependence on
total speech productivity. (b) Range of oral vocabulary tended to be relatively independent of other
language measures and showed a positive relationship
to social class level. While the higher social class
group demonstrated a wider range of oral vocabulary
than did the lower class group, this relationship
was not maintained when differences in IQ score were
controlled. (c) The mean sentence length measure
was related to social class level among younger
children but not among the older group. Lower class
first graders tended to use shorter sentences than a
comparable age group of higher social class subjects. (d) At the fifth grade level the race variable was related to intelligence, reading skill, and
sound discrimination test scores but not to the language measures of this research. At the first grade
level, the race variable was related to neither the
language nor the other test measures.

3. The content of children's speech obtained in
a relatively unstructured adult-child testing situation was, in general, not significantly influenced
by variables of sex, race, or social class level.
Older children, who talked considerably more than
the younger children did within a specified period
of time, were found to cover a wider range of topics
rather than to discuss any one topic more fully than
did the younger group.

4. The results of this research, compared with
those of previous studies, suggest that the appearance of sex differences in language performance is
highly dependent on the age and social class level
of the subject and on the specific linguistic skill
measured.

5. Where social class or racial differences in
language performance appeared, they were usually
found in conjunction with differences in performance
on the Lorge-Thorndike IQ tests. The language performance of fifth grade children, compared with that
of first grade subjects, was somewhat more sensitive

to the influence of social class and race variables."

(Authors' Summary)

C

Deutsche, Jean M., 1943.
The development of children's concepts of causal
relations.
In R. Barker, J. Kounin, and H. Wright (Eds.),
Child behavior and development,
New York: McGraw-Hill, Pp. 129-145.

This was an investigation of children's concepts of causal relations. The research used the
theoretical framework of Piaget as a basis. Subjects were 732 children in grades 3 to 8 from
varying social classes. Two types of instrument
were employed. Form I consisted of presentation
of experiments such as usually studied in physical
science. Form II consisted of a series of
questions dealing with natural phenomena, for
example, "What causes thunder?" Children's
responses were rated on accuracy of response
(explanations). Types of causality were also
examined.

The main findings included:
1. For all age groups, boys scored higher than
   girls on Form I.
2. There was no consistent difference in performance by social class.
3. Phenomenistic-type explanations decreased
   with age, from 37 per cent at 8 years to 10
   per cent at 16 years.
4. Logical deduction-type explanations increase
   with age, from 11 per cent at 8 years to 36
   per cent at 16 years.

F,D,A

Douglas, J. W. B., 1964.
The home and the school.
London: McGibbon and Kee.

This book is one of a series reporting data from
an extensive longitudinal study of a sample of all

children born in the first week of March, 1946, in
England. The 5,000 subjects included all children
born into middle-class families, one-fourth of all
those born into working-class families, and all
those born into agricultural families.

Data for the entire study include information
regarding birth, all doctors' reports throughout
childhood, and reports of social workers and home
visitors. Parents were questioned at intervals
regarding aspirations and expectations for their
children. Tests were individually administered to
children at age 8. These tests included a picture
intelligence test, vocabulary tests, reading, and
arithmetic tests. Students were retested at age
11 on arithmetic, reading, and verbal intelligence.
School records were also utilized.

In this book primary attention is focused on the
test performance of children at ages 8 and 11 and
the relationships between performance, school attended and its policies, and the home. Class differences in test performance based on a composite
score were found at both ages 8 and 11, with the
middle-class children scoring higher. For children
in the intermediate IQ range, school policy regarding streaming students by ability, and interest of
the parents in education were found to be decisive
in the attainment of grammar school places at age 11.

Considerable discussion is devoted to the
policies now operating in the English system and
to possible waste of talent because of an overly
selective school system.

D,F,E,A
Dreger, R. M. and Miller, K., 1960.
Comparative psychological studies of Negroes and
whites in the United States.
Psychol. Bull., 57, 361-402.

This is a critical review of published psychological studies during the period 1943-1958. The
authors found:

1. After equating for socio-economic variables, differences in measures of psychomotor functions tend to disappear.
2. Intelligence differences are reported, although comparisons of infants and young children suggest greater similarities in the early years. The reviewers point out many difficulties in these comparisons.
3. In temperament studies, differences are found but there is insufficient evidence to determine the basis for them. Likenesses in psychodynamics appear more typical than differences.
4. Religious values were ranked highest by Negroes and white females.
5. In general, there is much similarity in the value systems of whites and Negroes.
6. Differences in self-concepts are marked, being less adequate in Negroes.
7. "In the areas of psychological functioning most closely related to the sociological, social class differences show up more clearly as bases for differentiation between the two groups. Leadership, family life, child-rearing practices, fertility, and mate selection all seem to conform to social structure rather than to racial lines per se."
8. There is a higher incidence of mental illness among Negroes than among whites.
9. Educational achievement of Negroes relative to whites follow the pattern of intelligence-test differences.

D,F,E,B,A

Eells, K., 1953.
Some implications for school practice of the Chicago studies of cultural bias in intelligence tests.
Harvard educ. Rev., 23, 284-297.

An attempt was made to clarify the basic nature of cultural bias in intelligence tests and its relation to the school's objectives. The cultural-bias problem is that "most presently used intelligence tests...are so constructed and so

administered that scores on them are influenced by
the cultural backgrounds of the children taking
the test in such a way that children from certain
kinds of cultural backgrounds receive scores that
are not accurate reflections of their basic
intelligence."

The question of bias is irrelevant if intelligence is defined as the ability to do school
work, but then tests should be regarded as tests of
scholastic aptitude to avoid misunderstanding and
improper labeling and grouping. Intelligence is
defined by Eels in terms of problem-solving ability
as applied to problems which seem real and
important to the individual and under conditions
of maximum motivation. Since culture-free tests
are out of the question, culture-fair tests must
be constructed which measure fairly the basic
problem-solving ability of children from different
kinds of cultural backgrounds. To be free of
bias, a test must be composed of items which deal
with materials common to the various subcultures,
use common language, and stimulate equal degrees
of interest and motivation in the various subcultures in which it is used.

E,A

Empey, L., 1956.
Social class and occupational aspiration: a com-
parison of absolute and relative measurements.
Amer. sociol. Rev., 21, 703-709.

This was a study of the extent to which the
child is influenced in his aspirations by the
status of his father. The sample consisted of 764
subjects--or one-tenth of all male seniors--in
public high schools in the state of Washington
during the spring of 1954. Stratification for 10
levels of social class was based on fathers'
occupation.

The author found that:
1. The absolute occupational-status aspirations
   of male high school seniors is related to
   social-class status.

2. Lower-class senior boys aspire to and anticipate significantly higher occupational status than that of their fathers.
3. The relative aspiration, preferred compared to anticipated occupations, was comparable for lower-class boys and for higher-class boys.

It was concluded that lower-class youth do aspire to "get ahead," but do not aspire to the same absolute levels as do higher-status youth.

D,A

Fowler, W. L., 1957.
A comparative analysis of pupil performance on conventional and culture-controlled mental tests.
Fourteenth Yearbook of the National Council on Measurements in Education.
Princeton, N. J.: Educ. Test. Serv., 8-20.

This study contrasted three conventional with three culture-controlled mental tests by comparing pupil-test performance with sex, race, ethnic background, socio-economic status, and teacher estimate of pupil intelligence.

Subjects were 201 white American non-ethnics, 70 Negroes, and 84 Polish boys and girls, a total of 355 ten-year-old students from 18 schools. Eighteen teachers each rated a different group of subjects in the rank order of presumed intelligence. The tests administered to all were: California Short-Form Test of Mental Maturity, Detroit Alpha Intelligence Test, Henmon-Nelson Tests of Mental Ability, 2 IPAT Culture-Free tests (Cattell) and the Davis-Eells Games.

The culture-controlled tests did not show differences between the sexes, but the girls were superior to the boys on the Henmon-Nelson and the Detroit Alpha. Negro pupils generally scored lower than either of the two white groups. Socio-economic status (as measured by the Warner Index of Status Characteristics) was found to be positively related to test performance, except for the Polish group and the Negro boys. The type of test used did not greatly alter the IQ obtained. For the Polish and the Negro boys, lower socio-economic status was associated with a higher score on the conventional and a poorer score on the culture-controlled tests. It was also found that teacher estimate of pupil intelligence corresponded most closely with conventional tests.

A,F,E

Gill, L. J. and Spilka, B., 1962.
Some non-intellectual correlates of academic achievement among Mexican-American secondary school students.
J. educ. Psychol., 53, 144-149.

"The purpose of this study was to determine personal and maternal correlates of academic achievement among Mexican-American secondary school students (Juniors and Seniors)."

Four groups of 15 students each were matched on age, IQ, grade level, and courses taken. High achievers were above 70th percentile on grade-point average, and low achievers were below 30th percentile on grade-point average; boys and girls were compared as separate groups. Intelligence was assessed by the Otis Test of Mental Ability; grade-point averages were based on academic courses common to all subjects and emphasized verbal and symbolic skills. A modified version of the Parent Attitude Survey was used to measure dominating, possessive, and ignoring attitudes of mothers toward their offspring. The California Personality Inventory was used to assess achievement by conformance, achievement by independence, intellectual effectiveness, and resourcefulness and social maturity. Additional personality measures of hostility and adaptation to anxiety were also used.

The findings show no significant difference between mothers of high and low achievers on either possessive or ignoring attitudes. On conformity achievement high-achieving girls were significantly (.01) higher than high-achieving boys and, in general, high achievers were significantly higher than low achievers. Significant

112

differences (.05) were also found between high and low achievers on intellectual efficiency and social maturity. In general, high-achieving groups were less hostile and girls were less hostile than boys (.01 level of significance). Also, high-achieving groups showed more adaptable anxiety (.01 level of significance).

"It was conjectured that restrictive and demanding maternal attitudes are perceived by the achieving girls as affectional concern. However, in this ethnic group where the woman's role is inferior to the male's position, the male teenager may reject maternal domination and use poor school performance as a weapon against his demanding mother. The achieving student in this ethnic group has learned to conform to rules and regulations and to work under supervision. He does not appear to feel hostility toward authority figures such as teacher, because their demands have served as means for reward and personal satisfaction. Achieving girls apparently conform more than achieving boys or underachieving girls or boys."

E

Goff, R. M., 1954.
Some educational implications of the influence of rejection on aspiration levels of minority group children.
J. exp. Educ., 23, 179-183.

This study was concerned with the social pressure of rejection as it acts as a barrier to effective intellectual and social functioning of minority-group (Negro) children.

Sixty boys and 60 girls, ages 6 to 8 and 12 to 14, of high-income and low-income families in North Carolina were interviewed concerning successes and failure in out-of-school competitive activities, ranking of self in relation to school academic performance, ambitions, and wishes.

Findings:

1. Lower-income Negro children showed decreased confidence in out-of-school activities with increase in age.

2. Lower-income groups had more feelings of inadequacy in school. This feeling of inadequacy increased with age for the boys but not for the girls.

3. Upper-income Negro girls showed increased assurance with age in both school and out-of-school activities.

4. Lower-income girls felt least assured on self-esteem and least secure regarding probable success in the future.

5. Lower-income children believe money and lack of opportunity are major sources of interference with ambition, while upper-income children named ill health, bad luck, and death as possible factors interfering with realization of ambitions.

6. Children's wishes involve more material and concrete things than abstractions like happiness and health.

E,A

Goodman, Mary Ellen, 1952.
Race awareness in young children.
Cambridge: Addison-Wesley Press.

This was an investigation of awareness of race differences and feelings about such differences among young children. Negro and white children between the ages of 3-1/2 years and 5-1/2 years were studied. Fifty-seven of the children were Negroes and 46 were white. Stanford - Binet IQs ranged from 80 to 145.

Data were gathered by three persons who used the following means: non-participant observation, participant observation, interviewing, testing, and school records. All data were organized on a case-study basis. The data for each case were summarized and evaluated under the following two headings: (1) criteria for description and definition of awareness-attitude level, and (2) possible causes and correlates of awareness-attitude level.

Main findings:
1. "Four-year olds, particularly white ones, show unmistakable signs of the onset of racial bigotry."
2. "Negro children not yet five can sense that they are marked and grow uneasy."
3. "Higher levels of activity, emotionality, sensitiveness, gregariousness, competitiveness, and aggressiveness were observed among the Negro children compared with their white schoolmates."
4. "Race awareness comes from personal, social, and cultural experiences. The child picks up cues given by others."

The author concluded that "the very complexity of the process of attitude-generation in the early ages makes it possible to attack while the personality is still malleable, and even before the generation process is well under way."

G

Gottlieb, D., 1964.
Teaching and students: the views of Negro and white teachers.
Sociol. Educ., 37, 345-353.

This study attempted to identify similarities and differences between Negro and white elementary-school teachers and their views of their students and their work.

Eighty-nine teachers (53 white, 36 Negro) from six inner-city public schools which serve low-income Negro students were studied. The teachers were interviewed and responded to questionnaires regarding their backgrounds, and their views of teaching and their students. A check list of adjectives was used to describe students.

Major findings included:

1. The backgrounds of Negro and white teachers differ. Negro teachers come primarily from urban metropolitan areas and have non-professional fathers. In addition,

115

one-fourth of Negro teachers were raised in households with a female head. White teachers come primarily from medium-sized towns, with professional fathers.

2. Negro teachers express more satisfaction with their jobs in low-income schools than do the white teachers. Major reasons for job dissatisfaction on the part of the Negro teachers are problems of physical setting such as lack of materials and crowded classrooms. The white teachers, however, express dissatisfaction regarding lack of parental interest and behavior-discipline problems.

3. On the adjective check list, Negro teachers most often describe students as fun-loving, happy, co-operative, energetic, and ambitious, whereas white teachers view them as talkative, lazy, fun-loving, high strung, and rebellious.

The author suggests that teachers' backgrounds and expectations account for job satisfaction. Perhaps Negro teachers have greater personal investment in and identification with the students; therefore, they are dissatisfied with the educational system rather than with the students.

G,D

Gray, Susan W. and Klaus, R. A., 1963.
Interim report: early training project.
George Peabody College and Murfreesboro, Tenn.,
City Schools, Mimeo.

This is a report of the Early Training Project involving two experimental groups of approximately 20 Negro culturally deprived children each (T1: two summers of school program and home contact for intervening year, starting at approximately age 3 1/2; T2: one summer school program at approximately age 5) and two matched control groups. The program was aimed at improving attitudes toward achievement, and aptitudes and abilities (language, perception, concept formation) considered necessary for successful school learning.

116

Results of pre- and post-testing over a 15-month
period showed significantly greater improvement on
Binet and Peabody Picture Vocabulary Test for
experimental groups than for control groups.
Average IQ gain for experimental group T1 was 10.1
points (from 85.6 to 95.7) and for experimental
group T2 was 5.1 points (from 91.2 to 96.3). Control Group 1 showed average decrease of 5 points
(from 87.4 to 83.4) and Control Group 2 showed
decrease of 2.5 (from 88.0 to 85.5) over same
period of time.

D,E,C,A

Haggard, E. A., 1954.
Social status and intelligence: an experimental
study of certain cultural determinants of measured intelligence.
Genet. psychol. Monogr., 49, 141-186.

This study investigated the influence of social
status, practice, motivation, form of test, and
manner of presentation on intelligence-test performance under controlled conditions.

Subjects were drawn from the 11-year old
children of a midwestern city of 115,000. A total
of 671 children took part in the experiment. They
were subdivided into 28 subgroups of approximately
equal size, matched on social status (high and
low, as determined by the Index of Social
Characteristics), chronological age, school grade,
and IQ. The experiment was for 50 minutes a day
for five consecutive days. All subjects were
administered Initial Test of standard intelligence
test items on first day. Experimental conditions
involved Practice (motivated, unmotivated, and
none) for 3 days, and Retest (motivated and unmotivated) using Initial Standard Test and Revised
Test which minimized middle-class bias.

Major results:
1. Practice facilitated gain in performance of
    the high-status subjects who took the Standard
    Retest, and gain of the low-status subjects
    who took the Revised Retest.

2. Low-status subjects, when motivated, did significantly better on the Standard Retest than those not motivated.
3. Subjects from both social-status groups made much greater gains on the Revised than on the Standard Retest. The low-status subjects showed the greater gain.
4. Subjects from both status groups performed better on a Revised Initial Test than on the Standard Initial Test.
5. Even though the various experimental treatments and conditions influenced the retest scores differentially, when the effects of all treatments were combined, there was no significant difference between the two status groups in their ability to learn to solve intelligence-test problems.
6. The mere revision of the test items was not sufficient to reduce the difference in performance between the groups; the marked discrepancy between them was only decreased when the conditions of Motivation and Practice were also present. All the statistically significant differences attributable to Practice, Motivated Practice, and Motivated Retest occurred in connection with the Standard Retest; the Revised Retest was not influenced by such conditions.

It does not follow from the findings that adequate measures of mental ability can be obtained by merely revising current intelligence tests to remove their middle-class bias. This study demonstrated that if the individual or the group is not functioning with high motivation, or if efficient test-taking techniques have not been developed, or if rapport is not good, the resulting performance can readily be improved by improving these conditions.

G

Haubrich, V.`F., 1963.
The culturally different: new context for teacher education.
J. teacher Educ., 14, 163-167.

This is a description of a teacher training project at Hunter College to prepare teachers for "difficult" schools. The program assumes that training in these schools during student teaching with the option of permanent placement after graduation leads to better preparation of teachers for culturally deprived children.

Distinctive features of the training program included:
1. Student teachers volunteer for this placement.
2. Early in the semester the student handles two classes daily.
3. School personnel and college supervisor co-operate closely in supervision.
4. There is a regular program of visits to the community and its agencies and discussion of same.
5. There is a regular program for contact, observation, and discussion of school offices and personnel services.
6. School placement provides a direct means to enter teaching.

Over a two-year period, there were 32 volunteers of which 75 per cent elected to remain in the "difficult" schools as regular teachers.

E,D,A

Hieronymus, A. N., 1951.
Study of social class motivation: relationships between anxiety for education and certain socio-economic and intellectual variables.
J. educ. Psychol., 42, 193-205.

The purpose of this study was to determine the nature of the differences in social and economic expectations and attitudes toward education of high-school students representing different socio-economic groups.

119

Six hundred ten ninth-grade students of four six-
year high schools in a midwestern city were used as
the sample. Scales measuring socio-economic status,
attitude toward education, and level of socio-economic expectation were administered. Intelligence test
scores and performance scores on the Iowa Test of
Educational Development were obtained.

The author concluded that:
1. socio-economic status is more closely related
   to the level of socio-economic expectation
   than is test intelligence;
2. the relationship between socio-economic status
   and attitude toward education is about .30;
3. a high correlation exists between socio-economic expectation and attitude; and
4. a moderate relationship exists between the
   socio-economic expectation and attitude and
   composite scores on the Iowa Test of Educational Development.

D,B,A

Higgins, C. and Silvers, Cathryne M., 1958.
A comparison of the Stanford-Binet and the Colored
Raven Progressive Matrices IQ for children with low
socio economic status.
J. consult. Psychol., 22, 465-468.

This study tested the assumption that verbal
test items are more susceptible to degrees and
varieties of social exposure and cultural
deprivation, while non-verbal items are free of
this influence. It was hypothesized that for a
population of low socio-economic status, there
would be no significant differences between the
Stanford-Binet IQ and an IQ obtained from a non-
verbal test of intelligence.

Subjects were 789 pupils, from seven to nine
years of age, from a low socio-economic area,
tested individually with the Stanford-Binet, and
followed by the Colored Ravens Progressive
Matrices Test (CRPM).

Mean Stanford-Binet IQ for the 349 Negro subjects was 90.3; for the 440 white subjects,

90.6--the slight difference was not statistically significant.

The non-verbal CRPM showed differences by race, with scores for Negro children lower in all instances. For white children no significant difference was found between Stanford-Binet and CRPM measures. For the Negro group, however, the non-verbal scores were significantly lower than their verbal scores. The authors suggest that the CRPM may be measuring a very specific skill and is not a general intelligence test. They also suggest that tests constructed with many non-verbal items may be unfair to Negro children.

F,A

Hill, E. H. and Giammatteo, M. C., 1963.
Socio-economic status and its relationship to school achievement in the elementary school.
Elem. English, 40, 265-270.

This study investigated socio-economic status (SES) and its relationship to vocabulary, reading comprehension, arithmetic skills, problem-solving, and composite achievement scores.

The population studied was 223 third-grade children from western Pennsylvania. Socio-economic status was measured by an interview sheet. The Otis Quick-Scoring Mental Ability Test was used to measure ability. Iowa Tests of Basic Skills and the Scott-Foresman Reading Tests were used as achievement measures. Children were tested in third grade and their records obtained for first- and second-grade achievement data.

Correlations suggest that socio-economic status was an important factor in school achievement. The means obtained in basic skills indicated that children from the high SES group by grade 3 were eight months ahead of children from the low SES group in vocabulary achievement, nine months ahead in reading comprehension, six months ahead in arithmetic skills and eleven months ahead in problem solving. The average total achievement scores showed seven months' difference between the high

121

and lower SES groups. In the individual reading
tests, positive relationships were found between SES
and the reading subtests at both grade 1 and grade 3;
however, the relationship between SES and reading
subtests was significant at grade 1 and not at grade
3. Sensory imagery and phonetic analysis showed the
highest relationship with SES.

B,A

Irwin, O. C., 1948.
Infant speech. The effect of family occupational
status and of age on use of sound types.
J. speech hear. Disord., 13, 224-226.

Speech sound data were collected on two groups
of infants, one composed of children from homes of
laboring families, the other from homes of business, professional, and clerical families.
Children varying in age from 1 to 30 months were
studied. Data were analyzed for occurrence of
speech sounds (phoneme types).

Mastery of speech sounds for the two class
groups was found to progress at different rates.
Analysis of variance of the data indicated
significant differences with age and occupational
status. The older children and children from
higher-status homes produce more sound types. The
effect of social status seems particularly marked
in the older infants (1 1/2 to 2 1/2 years).

B,A

Irwin, O. C., 1948.
Infant speech. The effect of family occupational
status and of age on sound frequency.
J. speech hear. Disord., 13, 320-323.

Speech sound data were collected on two groups of
infants. One group was composed of babies from business, clerical, and professional homes; the other,
of babies from homes of laboring families. Data were
analyzed on the basis of phoneme frequency. Children ranged in age from 1 to 30 months.

122

Analysis of variance of the data indicated
significant effect of age for both occupational
groups; the older infants produced more sounds.
Differences between the occupational groups were
found to be negligible for the children under 1 1/2
year of age, but highly significant for children
1 1/2 to 2 1/2 years old. This result was similar
to the findings when sound types were used as the
criterion of speech development.

D,F,C

Jensen, A. R., 1963.
Learning ability in retarded, average and gifted
children.
Merrill-Palmer Q., 9 (2), 123-140.

This study attempted to determine how children
classified for educational purposes as "mentally
retarded" differ in their learning abilities from
children who are average or above average in
measured intelligence and scholastic aptitude.

Junior high school children classified as
"educationally mentally retarded" (N = 36;
Stanford-Binet IQs of 50-75) were compared on a
selective learning task with average (N = 24;
IQs 90-110) and gifted (N = 13; IQs above 135)
children in the same school. Mean ages were
approximately 14 years.

The task consisted of learning, by trial-and-
error, to associate 5 or 6 different stimuli
(colored geometric forms) with 5 or 6 different
responses (an array of pushbuttons). All groups
were given 2 tests, but special procedures were
used with the retarded individuals between the
first and second tests to make certain that they
understood the instructions and produced evidence
of learning. These procedures, variously used,
were verbal reinforcement by examiner, stimulus
naming, stimulus naming while learning, and delayed
response following reinforcement.

There were highly significant differences between the groups on the Index of Learning, and the
rate of learning correlated with IQ even in the

retarded group (.50 on the first test; .35 for the last test for this group). The author suggested that the highest correlation with IQ was on the first test probably because the ability to understand instructions, which played an important part in performance on the learning task, was also one of the crucial factors in the S-B intelligence scale. Variability was much greater among the retarded, who also showed much greater improvement with practice on successive forms of the learning task. Some of the retarded Ss learned as fast as the gifted. Adding verbal reinforcement and requiring Ss to verbalize (by naming the stimuli) while learning, resulted in marked improvement of the learning rate of some Ss. The results were discussed in terms of hypotheses involving as yet undiscovered "dimensions" of learning ability and in terms of the facilitative role of discriminative and mediating verbal behavior (especially "labeling") in learning.

The author concluded that since the retarded group spanned the entire range of learning ability as measured by the last test, a variety of learning tests which taps different dimensions would render a more complete and more highly refined diagnosis of the learning ability of children classified as mentally retarded than is afforded by standard intelligence tests. He also hypothesized that the normal and fast learners in the retarded group were not really retarded in a primary sense, but were children who, at some crucial period in their development, had failed to learn the kinds of behavior which are necessary as a basis for school learning and for the acquisition of the kinds of knowledge and skills tapped by IQ tests.

C,B,G

Jensen, A. R., 1963.
Learning in the pre-school years.
J. nursery Educ., 18 (2), 133-138.

A review of some studies in animal and human learning indicated the possibility that the amount and variety of verbal and sensory stimulation the organism experiences have considerable effect on learning behavior. For example: Rats raised in a stimulating environment (triangles and circles on cage walls) compared to a group raised in plain cages showed much more success in discrimination tasks (Gibson, 1956; Forgus, 1954).

Jensen studied the influence of exposure to an object with limited verbal contexts and exposure for the same amount of time with multiple verbal contexts. Twenty-month-old children who had been exposed to "doll" in many verbal contexts showed greater ability to discriminate object "doll" from many objects. In another experiment, children shown an object for an equal length of time with one group allowed to handle object and the other group receiving visual experience alone were compared. Learning was more rapid for group which received both visual and tactile experience.

The author also reviewed verbal mediation studies which indicate more rapid learning when task comes under verbal control. Implications for nursery education are discussed.

B,C,D,A

John, Vera P., 1963.
The intellectual development of slum children: some preliminary findings.
Amer. J. Orthopsychiat., 33, 813-822.

This study examined certain patterns of verbal and cognitive behavior in a sample of grade 1 and grade 5 Negro children from 3 social classes. Lower-lower class included parents who had 9 years of schooling or less with father absent in one-third of the families. Upper-lower class included semi-skilled parents who had attended high school with father absent in one-third of the families. Middle-class group included parents who had attended college and were professionals and civil servants; 4 per cent of the fathers were absent.

Sixty-nine first-grade and 105 fifth-grade children were administered tests which measured use of language. Tasks involving labeling, relating and categorizing were included.

Results showed differences between classes on
Peabody Picture Vocabulary Test, Enumeration, Integration, IQ, and WISC vocabulary were not significant
at grade 1 although trend with class was there. In
grade 5 there were no differences in Enumeration but
all other tests showed a significant difference in
favor of the middle class. On the sorting task,
fifth-grade lower-class children sort cards into more
piles and give significantly fewer explicit verbalizations of their sorting behavior than do the middle-
class children. In relational use of language group
differences were small.

The author concluded that "acquisition of more
abstract and integrative language seems to be
hampered by the living conditions in the homes
of lower-class children. Opportunities for
learning to categorize and integrate are rare in
the lives of all young children. This type of
learning requires specific feedback or careful
tutoring."

D,B,A

Jones, W. R., 1960.
A critical study of bilingualism and non-verbal in-
telligence.
Brit. J. educ. Psychol., 30, 71-77.

This study examined the influence of variables
other than the bilingual factor on non-verbal
intelligence-test performance, since other investigations (reviewed) had concluded that
bilingualism has an adverse effect on performance
in non-verbal tests.

Results from the 1951 Bangor Survey in
Caernarvonshire were re-analyzed in the light of
socio-economic data. All children between the ages
of 10 and 12 had been given a series (unspecified)
of tests and a Language Questionnaire and were
grouped as Welsh, Mixed-Welsh, Mixed-English, and
English. It had been found originally that there
was a tendency for mean raw scores on the non-
verbal test to increase as the linguistic
composition of the group became progressively more

126

English. A re-analysis of these data by occupational status showed that linguistic groups which had equivalent social status also had equivalent non-verbal intelligence test scores.

It was concluded that bilingualism is not necessarily a source of intellectual disadvantage. In studies of monoglot and bilingual children, status characteristics should always be examined.

A,E,F,D

Kahl, J. A., 1953.
Educational and occupational aspirations of 'Common Man' boys.
Harvard educ. Rev., 23, 186-203.

This was an interview study aimed at exploring the social influences which helped to account for differences in motivation to go on to college among high school boys of similar background and intelligence level.

Twenty-four boys and their parents were interviewed at some length. Twelve planned to go to college and 12 did not. All had IQs in the top three deciles. The parents regarded themselves as "common man." Fifteen of the families had as their core value "getting by," while 9 families believed in the core value of "getting ahead." About 27 per cent of the "getting by" families had boys who planned to go to college, while almost 90 per cent of the "getting ahead" families had boys who planned to go to college.

Parents who were discontented with their status tended to train their sons from the earliest years of school to take school seriously and to use education as the means to climb into the middle class. Only sons who internalized such values were sufficiently motivated to overcome the obstacles which faced the common man boys in school; only they saw a reason for good school performance and college aspirations.

C,F,D

Katz, Phyllis A. and Deutsch, M., 1963.
Relation of auditory-visual shifting to reading
achievement.
Percept. mot. Skills, 17, 327-332.

"One perceptual skill which may underlie reading
behavior is the ability to process sequentially
presented auditory and visual information. The
present study investigated the hypothesis that retarded and potentially retarded readers would
exhibit difficulty in rapidly shifting attention
between auditory and visual stimuli."

Reaction times to a series of lights (red and
green) and sounds (high and low) were obtained from
48 Negro male normal and retarded readers in Grades
1, 3, and 5. The interaction between type of reaction time (within one mode or across-modes) and
reading skill was significant at .01 level.

Data supported the hypothesis that shifting attention between modalities is more difficult for poor
readers. Another possible explanation for the data
is that the low group is poorer at response general-
ization, since the difference between the two groups
diminishes during second half of test period. Age
was found to be significantly associated with over-
all reaction time, with the older children reacting
faster. IQ was found to be unrelated to performance
on the task.

A,E,D,F

Keller, Suzanne, 1963.
The social world of the urban slum child: some
early findings.
Amer. J. Orthopsychiat., 33, 823-831.

This paper compared selected aspects of the
after-school and home activities of a sample of
poor Negro and Caucasian children currently
attending first and fifth grades in New York City
public schools.

Forty-six first- and fifth-grade Negro and
white students classified as upper-lower class

were tested, parents given questionnaires, and one-fifth of families interviewed in their homes.

The children came from large families living in relatively crowded and poor conditions. However, two-thirds of the parents believed they were coming up in the world; this expectation was reflected in the hopes they had for their children to graduate from college and enter a profession. The children had little sustained contact with adults, few organized conversations, and little shared family activity. It was suggested that constricted experience might account for the below normal IQ scores: on Lorge-Thorndike non-verbal test the mean in first grade was 97, and in fifth grade, 89.

Comparing Negroes and whites, lower-class Negro children came from larger families, and fewer of these children were supported by their father's earnings. Three times as many Negro as white children lived in families where adults were currently unemployed and receiving welfare or aid. White fathers had an average of one more year of schooling than Negro fathers, and white mothers had one-half year more than Negro mothers. In both groups mothers were better educated than fathers. Negro parents were geographically more mobile than whites, but less mobile occupationally.

Fifth-grade Negro children showed more negative self-evaluations than white children (80 per cent unfavorable self-other comparisons compared to 30 per cent for white children). Over half of the Negro fifth-graders were judged by their teachers to have little motivation, to be sad or pre-occupied, and working below capacity in school. Negro parents were very much concerned about their children's work, while nearly all white families were satisfied with their children's school performance.

D,F,A

Kennedy, A., Van De Riet, V., and White, J. C., Jr., 1963.
A normative sample of intelligence and achievement of Negro elementary school children in the south-eastern United States.
Soc. Res. Child Develpm. Monogr., 28, No. 6.

A review of the literature on Negro-white differences in intelligence indicates that Negroes typically score lower than the normative samples which exclude Negroes. It was felt that broad normative data on the Negro population are necessary to make intelligence-test findings more meaningful for individual psychologists and educators who perform diagnostic evaluations on Negro school children.

During the 1960-61 school year, a normative study of the intelligence and achievement of Negro elementary school children in 5 southeastern states was carried out. The sample of 1,800 represented two-thirds of a per cent of the children in the elementary-school age range in Florida, Georgia, Alabama, Tennessee, and South Carolina, evenly distributed between rural, urban, and metropolitan counties. The 1960 Revision, Form L-M, of the Stanford-Binet Intelligence Test and the 1957 Revision of the California Achievement Test (CAT) were administered. Means were computed according to grade, sex, age, teacher rating, and community size.

Total sample mean IQ was 80.7, standard deviation was 12.4, as compared with Terman and Merrill's data of a mean IQ of 101.8, S.D. 16.4. There was no significant trend in IQ from grades 1 through 6, but IQ was negatively correlated with age, for example, the 5-year-old group had a mean IQ of 86 as compared with the mean IQ of 65 for the 13-year-old group. IQ was significantly different by socio-economic level, upper level having a mean of 105 and lower a mean of 79. There were only slight mean differences between the IQs of metropolitan, urban, and rural children. IQ correlated .32 with teacher over-all

130

ratings. "Analysis of Binet item difficulty and biserial correlation item analysis showed that the abstract verbal items appear at too low an age level in the test. On the other hand, rote memory, days of the week, making change, digits, and sentence memory items are placed too high on the scale. There does not seem to be any exceptionally high performance ability in contrast to low verbal ability for this sample."

Results from the CAT indicate an increase in the discrepancy between the mean of the Negro sample at each grade level and the mean of the normative sample used to standardize the test. CAT results were reported according to socio-economic level. The results showed a trend of proportionate decrease in achievement level as one goes down the socio-economic scale. Also, girls tended to score higher than boys at each level. No significant trends were observed between CAT and community size. A correlation of .69 was obtained between Binet MA and CAT.

D,F

Kirk, S. A., 1958.
Early education of the mentally retarded.
Urbana: University of Illinois Press.

This book reports an investigation of the influence of nursery school-like experience on the intelligence of feeble-minded children. Subjects were 81 retarded children between 3 and 6 years old. Twenty-eight children attended a special nursery school; 15 institutionalized children attended an institution nursery school; controls who did not attend nursery school were matched for place of residence (institution or not institution), IQ, and socio-economic status. IQ testing was done initially, after nursery experience, and follow-up three to five years later.

Evidence was presented both as case studies and group comparisons. The main finding was that the over-all effect of the nursery experience on retarded children was positive. Of the 43 retarded children who had nursery experience, 30 (70 per

131

cent) showed an acceleration in rates of intellectual growth, ranging from 10 to 30 IQ points.
Increase for experimental group was significantly
higher (.05) than that for controls. Six of the
15 institutionalized children improved sufficiently to allow placement in the community in
foster homes. Moreover, the children retained the
accelerated rates of growth established during the
nursery-school experience during the follow-up
period of from three to five years.

B,D

Kirk, S. A. and McCarthy, J. J., 1961.
The Illinois Test of Psycholinguistic Abilities --
an approach to differential diagnosis.
Amer. J. ment. Def., 66, 399-412.

A battery of nine tests of psycholinguistic
abilities is described, together with four profiles and brief histories to illustrate
possibilities of application. The theoretical
model from which the tests were derived bears some
relationship to Osgood's models in communication
theory and psycholinguistics, and to Wepman's
model for aphasia. The test is a diagnostic
instrument to provide information for remediating
deficits in various psycholinguistic functions.
The authors emphasize extending this type of
behavior diagnosis to individually prescribed
remedial teaching situations.

The test includes measures of modes of input
and output (visual-auditory input; vocal-motor
output); levels of organization (automatic-
sequential, representational or meaning level);
and psycholinguistic processes (decoding, en-
coding, and association).

D,F,A

Klineberg, O., 1935.
Negro intelligence and selective migration.
New York: Columbia University Press.

The purpose of this investigation was to determine whether the superiority of northern over
southern Negroes on intelligence tests is due to

132

selective factors in migration or to a more stimulating environment in the North.

A comparison was made between the intellectual level of those who left the South and those who stayed behind. An examination of school records in Nashville, Birmingham, and Charleston was made to see whether those children who had migrated to the North represented in their schoolwork a superior group in relation to the total Negro school population in those cities. About 1,000 records were examined and it was found that migrating children did not differ regularly or consistently from their non-migrating classmates in school marks.

A second method used was to give intelligence and performance tests to southern-born Negro children living in New York, comparing the groups with different lengths of residence in New York. About 3,000 children were involved in 9 distinct studies. It was found that the scores of the migrants on the Stanford-Binet and the National Intelligence test increased fairly regularly with increasing length of residence in New York, and tended with time to approximate those of the New York-born. However, on the Otis Self-Administering Test there was no clear pattern of improvement associated with length of residence in New York, which was also true for other performance tests.

The author concluded that the superiority of the northern Negroes to the southern Negroes is not due to selective migration but to factors in the environment.

D,F,A

Klineberg, O., 1963.
Negro-white differences in intelligence test performance: a new look at an old problem.
Amer. Psychologist, 18, 198-203.

This is an attempt to bring up to date an analysis of the problem of Negro-white differences in intelligence test performance. There is no question that, on the average, Negro children obtain lower scores than whites (Shuey, 1958, on the basis of a review of 72 studies estimates the average IQ to be 85), but the crucial issue is that comparisons are permissible only when the environmental differences are absent or negligible. The 3 major studies cited by Shuey (Bruce, 1940; McGurk, 1951; Tanser, 1939) as demonstrating that differences persist even when environmental factors have been "equated" are criticized on the ground that equating on a socio-economic scale cannot be regarded as taking care of all the relevant environmental variables.

Evidence is cited to disprove the assumption of native differences in intelligence and to illustrate the positive effects of improved educational environments on the IQs of Negro children (Pasamanick, 1946; Araston and D'Angelo, 1952; Key, 1932; Klineberg, 1935; Clark, 1923; Lee, 1951; Stallings, 1960). It is further pointed out that there is a great deal of overlap in scores and that group differences are obscure, uncertain, and do violence to the facts of individual capacities and potentialities. The author concludes that the view that ethnic groups differ in innate abilities is not supported by any scientifically acceptable evidence.

D, E

Klugman, S. F., 1944.
The effect of money incentives vs. praise upon the reliability and obtained scores of the Revised Stanford-Binet test.
J. gen. Psychol., 30, 255-267.

The author investigated two problems. Would children obtain higher scores on the Revised Stanford-Binet (S-B) if the incentive of a monetary reward was employed in place of praise? Would the reliability of the test be improved by this incentive?

Thirty-eight white and 34 Negro school children in grades 2 to 7, ages 7 to 14, were tested with one form of the Revised S-B and a week later with the other. Scores on the initial testing were 99.11 and 98.00, respectively, for the two races. Money was used as the incentive in half the cases; praise in the other. Children were divided on the basis of race, sex, age, and father's occupation for investigating the effects of the incentives.

It was found that the reliability coefficients for those tested with money incentives were not significantly higher. All subgroups studied (race, sex, age, grade, and father occupation) obtained higher mean scores on the money incentive tests than on praise, but differences were not statistically significant. There was, however, a significant superiority of the scores of Negro children when tested with money incentives (99.56) over Negroes tested with praise incentives (96.16). Also, although there was practically no difference between whites and Negroes when money was the incentive, the whites showed superiority when praise was the incentive.

D,F

Knief, Lotus M. and Stroud, J. B., 1959. Intercorrelations among various intelligence, achievement, and social class scores. J. educ. Psychol., 50, 117-120.

The purpose of this study was to provide additional data on the social class or cultural bias in intelligence testing and to ascertain interrelationships among certain relatively new intelligence tests and scholastic achievement.

The Lorge-Thorndike Intelligence Tests (verbal and non-verbal), Davis-Eells Games, Iowa Tests of Basic Skills (ITBS), and the Warner Index of Status Characteristics were given to a sample of 344 fourth-grade pupils in a midwestern city. The Raven Progressive Matrix (RPM) was given the following year to 164 of these pupils.

All the intelligence tests used and the ITBS composite scores correlated significantly with social status and to approximately the same degree

(.30 to .34), except for RPM (.17). Multiple
correlation analysis showed that L-T verbal gave
the best prediction of Iowa Basic Skills scores,
followed by L-T non-verbal and Davis-Eells
Games. The RPM had the smallest correlation with
the Iowa. The authors conclude that for general
predictive purposes, the L-T verbal seems most
appropriate and the other tests used are probably
not adequate for prediction of achievement.

A
Kohn, M. L., 1959.
Social class and the exercise of parental authority.
Amer. sociol. Rev., 24, 252-266.

The conditions under which middle- and working-
class parents punish their pre-adolescent children
physically, or refrain from doing so, appear to be
quite different. Working-class parents are more
likely to respond in terms of the immediate consequences of the child's actions, middle-class
parents in terms of their interpretation of the
child's intent in acting as he does. This reflects differences in parents' values: Working-
class parents value for their children qualities
that assure respectability; desirable behavior
consists essentially of not violating pro-
scriptions. Middle-class parents value the child's
development of internalized standards of conduct;
desirable behavior consists essentially of acting
according to the dictates of one's own principles.
The first necessarily focuses on the act itself,
the second on the actor's intent.

[These conclusions were based on an interview
study of 200 white working-class and 200 white
middle-class families with children in the fifth
grade.]

(Author's Summary)

136

Kohn, M. L. and Carroll, Eleanor E., 1960.
Social class and the allocation of parental respon-
sibilities.
Sociometry, 23, 372-392.

The purpose of the study was to examine "the effects of middle- and working-class parents' ideolo-
gies of child rearing upon the division, between
mother and father, of responsibilities for the support and constraint of the children." Data concerning parents' and children's assessments of how
these responsibilities should be, and are, in fact,
allocated were obtained.

The sample included 200 representative white
working-class and 200 white middle-class families,
each with a child in the fifth grade. Interviews
were conducted with all the mothers and with a
fourth of the fathers and children.

The results indicated that "Middle-class mothers
emphasize the father's obligation to be as
supportive as the mother herself; his role in im-
posing constraints is of only secondary importance.
Working-class mothers would have their husbands be
more directive; the father's responsibility to
play a major part in the imposition of constraints
assumes far greater importance." While middle-
class fathers tend to share their wives'
conception of how responsibilities should be
allocated, at least with regard to sons, working-
class fathers feel that child rearing is the
wife's responsibility.

G,F,E,B

Krugman, M., 1961.
The culturally deprived child in school.
Nat. Educ. Ass. J., 50, 22-23.

In this review article, the effects of cultural
deprivation were studied by noting the deficit in
IQ and reading-test scores for children in a large,
low socio-economic district of New York City. In
comparing third-graders with sixth- and eighth-
graders, the deficit was seen to be cumulative or
increasing with time.

Several experimental programs being tried in New York City were reviewed. Some of the facets of these programs follow:

1. Individual psychological examinations, non-verbal intelligence tests, and subjective rating procedures were used rather than group intelligence tests.

2. Concentration of effort was in the elementary grades because results are obtainable there at lower costs, since deficit is not so great and there are fewer negative attitudes toward education.

3. Programs produced changed self-concepts by giving children "the feeling that the school cared" and by having the children succeed. These changes were accompanied by higher levels of aspiration and better adjustment.

4. Remedial services, individual and small group, were provided with special emphasis on written and spoken English.

5. Guidance and counseling services were combined with intensive instruction so that students could recognize the need for exerting efforts to succeed.

6. Opportunities for cultural experiences--trips to museums, theaters, scientific laboratories, and libraries--were provided and supplemented by classroom activities.

It was concluded that schools can compensate for the inadequate backgrounds that children from deprived homes bring to the classroom.

G

Larson, R. and Olson, J. L., 1963.
A method of identifying culturally deprived kindergarten children.
Except. Children, 30, 130-134.

This article describes an attempt at systematically identifying culturally deprived children. Four hypotheses constituted the theoretical structure used for discrimination purposes. Hypotheses dealt with language development, self-concept, social skills, and cultural differences.

138

A battery of tests was assembled to be used for evaluation, selection, and information purposes. Tests were administered to 250 kindergarten children in Racine, Wisconsin. An experimental group and a control group of children were selected on the basis of this battery. Curriculum plans are being made on the basis of the test results and continued evaluation will be carried out through the children's first years in school.

The battery included the following:
Language Development: Illinois Test of Psycholinguistic Abilities, Metropolitan Readiness Test, tape recordings, Binet vocabulary, Symbol Recognition Test (familiar objects), teacher screening device, and Body Type-Self Measure.
Self-Concept: Impossible Questions (frustration task), Sex and Race-Self Measure, House-Tree-Person Drawings, and teacher screening.
Social Skills: parent questionnaire (home activities), teacher screening.
Cultural Differences: parent questionnaire, teacher screening, General Information Test (child's knowledge of immediate environment), enrollment form, and Stanford-Binet IQ.

Comment: An exceptionally fine attempt at systematic identification of culturally deprived children based on extensive use of research results.

D,A

Lee, E. S., 1951.
Negro intelligence and selective migration: A Philadelphia test of the Klineberg hypothesis. Amer. sociol. Rev., 16, 227-233.

The purpose of this study was to investigate the relationship between intelligence test scores of Negro children and the length of time spent in northern schools, by analyzing re-test scores of the same children after varying periods of northern residence.

The basic groups of Negro children studied consisted of 212 Philadelphia-born children who had attended kindergarten, 424 who had not attended kindergarten, and 930 migrants from the South who were divided into 5 classes, according to the grade in which they entered the Philadelphia school system. Mean IQs from the Philadelphia Tests of Mental and Verbal Ability from initial tests and subsequent retests (grades 1, 2, 4, 6, and 9) were compared.

It was found that the group which had attended kindergarten averaged consistently higher than the group which entered the first grade with no pre-school experience. Within each of the Philadelphia-born groups there was no consistent tendency for scores to rise upon retesting, but in each of the groups that had migrated to the city, there was a significant tendency for mean scores to improve with increasing length of northern residence. The earlier the entry, the higher the IQs in any one grade. The Primary Mental Abilities Test and the Minnesota Paper Form Board were also administered to some of the children to determine whether improvement in general intelligence was associated with specific abilities. Again it was found that test scores and length of residence in Philadelphia were highly related except for PMA Memory test.

E,A

Le Shan, L. L., 1952.
Time orientation and social class.
J. abnorm. soc. Psychol., 47, 589-592.

The hypothesis investigated in this paper is that temporal goal orientations vary by social class. Lower-lower class orientation is conceived of as quick sequences of tension and relief, with little planning for the future. Time orientation in the upper-lower, middle and lower-upper classes is one of longer tension-relief sequences and planning further into the future as the individual grows older.

The author presented a re-examination of certain
child-rearing data which confirms the expectation
that training in these social classes is consistent
with the hypothesis. Lower-lower-class families
tend to train children with immediate punishments
and rewards. Families of the upper-middle, middle,
and lower-upper classes tend to stress the future,
and punishment and reward are often deferred.

Children 8 to 10 years old were asked to tell a
story to the examiner. Seventy-four children were
lower class and 43 were middle class. Stories of
middle-class children were found to contain a
longer time period for action than those of lower-
class children. The difference was significant at
.001 level.

The author concluded that time orientation
varies systematically with social class and
suggested this factor should be considered in
educational efforts with lower-class children.

E,A

Lott, A. J. and Lott, Bernice E., 1963.
Negro and white youth.
New York: Holt, Rinehart and Winston, Inc.

The aim of this study was to explore the values
and goals of Negro and white youth in areas most
relevant to their educational and vocational
choices and plans. Senior classes of four Kentucky
community high schools (two rural and two urban,
two Negro and two white) were studied. Total
sample was 301 students. Subjects were tested
with a Goal Preference Inventory to measure needs
(academic recognition, social recognition, and
love and affection needs), a modified form of the
Study of Values, a Background and Outlook
questionnaire, a Leadership Poll, and French's
Test of Insight which measures achievement and
affiliation motives. In addition, student leaders
in each school were interviewed.

Some of the main findings follow:
1. White students have greater economic and
   general home stability than Negro students.

2. For both Negroes and whites religious, social, and theoretical values are more important than economic, political, or aesthetic values.
3. No reliable differences were found between Negro and white groups with respect to affiliation motive. The dominant life goals for both groups are the desire for popularity, desire to achieve success, attain security, and obtain knowledge.
4. Negro youth view the future with optimism and more positively than white youth despite their awareness of discrimination and prejudice.
5. The socio-economic background of leaders is somewhat higher than that of other students. Negro leaders have fathers who are better educated than the fathers of most Negro students.
6. Leaders from both groups are more person-oriented, value religious pursuits, have high affiliation motive, high achievement motive, and are more verbal than non-leaders.
7. Negro leaders are more motivated to achieve financial security and respectability, while white leaders aim toward more idiosyncratic and inner sources of satisfaction.
8. Sex differences in values and patterns of motivation are more marked in the white group than the Negro group.

A,E

Lynn, D. B. and Sawrey, W. L., 1959.
The effects of father-absence on Norwegian boys and girls.
J. abnorm. soc. Psychol., 59, 258-262.

To examine the effect of father-absence on boys as compared with that on girls, the authors studied 40 father-absent families and 40 father-present families in Norway. All families had about the same social status level. The absent fathers were sailors and whalers who were away about 9 months of each year. An interview and a Structured Doll Play

test was used for the children who were in the
early level of primary education.

The authors found:
1. More father-absent boys than father-present
   boys showed immaturity.
2. Father-absent boys showed stronger striving
   toward father identification than father-
   present boys.
3. Father-absent boys showed more compensatory
   masculinity.
4. Father-absent boys had poorer peer adjustment than father-present boys or father-
   absent girls.
5. Father-absent girls were more dependent on
   the mother than father-present girls.

It was concluded that absence of the father does
affect the personality development of children.
However, other factors may also be involved, such
as the kind of woman who marries a sailor.

A

MacDonald, M., McGuire, C., and Havighurst, R.,
1949.
Leisure activities and the socio-economic status of
children.
Amer. J. Sociol., 54, 505-519.

This study examined leisure activities of
children from varying socio-economic groups. The
sample was 241 fifth-, sixth-, and seventh-
graders (ages 10-12) in an urban public school.
Socio-economic status was determined by father's
occupation and type of housing. Activities were
reported and categorized, and comparisons were
made among four social classes.

Differences were found in the leisure-time
activities of children in the four social classes.
Middle-class children took part mainly in Scouts
and YMCA, while lower-class children were active
primarily in centers for "underprivileged
children." Significant differences were found in
the number of activities within the family: the
highest stratum had the most family activity. The

number of persons who read books and listened to the radio increased from the lowest to the highest stratum. Those in the lower strata attended significantly more movies than did those in the upper strata. A few exceptions occurred in which lower-class children participated in middle-class organizations with middle-class children, apparently learning attitudes and habits leading toward upward mobility.

D,F,E

McBee, G. and Duke, R. L., 1960.
Relationship between intelligence, scholastic motivation, and academic achievement.
Psychol. Rep., 6, 3-8.

The effect of intelligence and scholastic motivation and the inter-relationships of these factors with academic achievement were investigated.

Tests of intelligence (California Test of Mental Maturity), scholastic motivation (scale from the Brown-Holtzman Survey of Study Habits and Attitudes), and academic achievement (Sequential Tests of Educational Progress and the California Tests of Achievement) were administered to seventh-grade students. Scores from the CTMM and the Scholastic Motivation scale were used as criteria for selection of 180 subjects, grouped in 3 levels of intelligence and 3 levels of motivation.

The analysis indicated a strong positive relationship between intelligence and achievement. The relationship between scholastic motivation and achievement appeared to be a significant factor in the areas of arithmetic, reading, and science, but not in language function and social studies. The relationship between intelligence and motivation was found to be additive rather than multiplicative, that is, an increase in scholastic motivation resulted in about the same increase in performance regardless of level of mental functioning.

D,C,B,A

McCandless, B., 1952.
Environment and intelligence.
Amer. J. ment. Defic., 56, 674-691.

The author discusses the essential nature of environment both in the development and the maintenance of intellectual functioning. He adopts a learning point of view to discuss evidence gathered from studies done on preschool children, children from different social classes, foster children, and mental defectives. He concludes that it seems likely that intelligence level may be a function of the amount of material available for learning and the types of learning which occur.

The bright individuals have rich opportunities to learn intellectually and opportunities to attain relatively constructive expectancies (that is, the child is richly equipped verbally to incorporate his environment, and increases progressively in power to handle it and achieve success). Dull children have a paucity of learning experiences of a constructive intellectual sort. The "performance" skew of the lower socio-economic class child progressively limits him; he is without tools to assimilate to the same degree new experiences and becomes increasingly more concrete and inflexible in his intellectual power. The dull child does learn self-defeating behaviors, expectancies of failure, absolute as opposed to abstract thinking, belief in his essential unworthiness, and a perceived failure to reach a goal. The various frustrations experienced by the culturally deprived child are seen as interfering with his problem-solving ability.

B,A

McCarthy, Dorothea, 1930.
Language development of the preschool child.
Inst. Child. Welf. Monogr., No. 4, Minneapolis.

This is a report of an investigation of the acquisition of speech by children in the preschool years. Subjects were between 18 and 54 months of age. One hundred forty children, 20 at each of

seven age levels, were selected as representative
of the occupational distribution in Minneapolis on
the basis of the father's occupation. Children
were observed at home or in nursery school alone
with investigator. Fifty consecutive spontaneous
verbal responses were recorded for each child
while he played or looked at picture books. A
response was a unit of speech preceded and followed
by pauses.

Mean length of response for every age group was
found to be significantly higher for higher socio-
economic status (SES) children than for lower SES
children. Using Piaget's functional analysis in
relation to paternal occupation, children from
upper SES were found to use a larger percentage of
adapted-information responses and ask more
questions than the children of lower SES.

D,A

McGehee, W. and Lewis, W. D., 1942.
Socio-economic status of the homes of mentally
superior and retarded children and the rank of
their parents.
Pedagogical Seminary, 60, 375-380.

The authors maintained that most investigations
of social class and intelligence fail to emphasize
the many exceptions reported in their data, and are
open to question because of techniques used in
securing subjects, or because of the limited geo-
graphic area or number of cases from which subjects
were drawn.

Subjects were drawn from a population of approximately 45,000 children in grades 4 to 8 in 455
schools, in 310 communities, and in 36 states. The
upper and lower 10 per cent of these on Kuhlmann-
Anderson test, plus a third group selected at random
representing the average child were studied. IQ was
correlated with socio-economic status information
(Terman-Taussig and modified Sims Score Card).
(Superior N = 4,176; Average, N = 12,390; Retarded,
N = 3,697).

Data showed positive relation between intelligence and father occupation-SES, but authors emphasized that superior and retarded children were found at all levels and showed that the great bulk of superior and retarded children came from "average" homes. Authors concluded that positive relationships between SES and mental ability hold primarily when group averages are considered and that a knowledge of the parent's occupation or SES conditions of the home is a very precarious index of the child's intelligence.

E,A

McKee, J. P. and Leader, F. B., 1955.
The relationship of socio-economic status and aggression to the competitive behavior of pre-school children.
Child Develpm., 26, 135-141.

The authors investigated the following hypotheses: (a) Competitive behavior will appear earlier and be more intense among children from lower socio-economic origins. (b) A substantial positive correlation between competition and aggression exists. (c) With older subjects aggression will be more common among lower socio-economic groups.

Fifty-six pairs of 3- and 4-year-old children equally divided as to sex, age, and socio-economic status (family income) were tested in an experimental play situation. The sample was first pre-tested and then matched. The children's behavior and verbalizations were rated for degree of competition and degree of aggression. Competition was defined as behavior the intent of which is to excel. Aggression was defined as behavior the intent of which is to injure. The authors noted that the lower-status children in this study were lower-middle class according to Warner's scale.

The major findings included:
1. A low correlation was found between competition and aggression (r = +.22).

2. Significantly more competition was found among children from lower socio-economic origins than among children from upper-middle socio-economic origins.
3. More instances of competition occurred among older children than among younger children and among boys than girls.
4. Aggression was more common among the lower-status children.
5. Sex and age differences in aggression did not appear.

A,E

Maas, H. S., 1951.
Some social class differences in the family systems and group relations of pre- and early adolescents. Child Develpm., 22, 145-152.

The purpose of this study was to propose a re-interpretation of some social behavioral patterns of pre- and early adolescents in lower-class and core-culture families.

Twenty-one subjects were studied as the sample. Parents and peers were interviewed to determine the subjects' relations with parents, siblings, and peers; no quantitative data were reported.

The results included observation of psychologically closed and quite rigid parental relationships with children in the lower class. The core-culture children were reported as experiencing a more open and flexible parental relationship. Lower-class children expressed fear of parental authority and were characterized as either prototypes of the "bully" or oversubmissive followers. The core-culture children were reported as not seeming to fear or to identify with threatening power of adults. Lower-class parents were reported as closed or in-accessible to the child's communication, core-culture parents as open to communication. The peer relations of lower-class children were classified into two types of security-seeking relationships: in one, the child identified with power and needed peers to establish his high status in relation to his contemporaries; in the other the child seemed dependent on the physical presence of peers for mutual succorance and direction. In core-culture peer groups a much less dependent relationship among siblings and peers was reported.

A,B

Milner, Esther, 1951.
A study of the relationship between reading readiness in grade one school children and patterns of parent-child interactions.
Child Develpm., 22, 95-122.

This study investigated certain parent-child interaction patterns as related to reading readiness of first-grade children. The subjects for the study were 42 first-grade children who were identified as high and low scorers on reading readiness. Interviews were conducted with the children and their mothers.

All high scorers but one were in the middle and upper classes; all low scorers but one were in the lower classes. Interview results indicate that high scorers have a much richer verbal environment than low scorers: there are more books in the home; the children are read to more often; they speak with parents at meals and at other times. Low scorers are subjected to physical punishment much more often than higher scorers.

E

Mischel, W., 1961.
Preference for delayed reinforcement and social responsibility.
J. abnorm. soc. Psychol., 62, 1-7.

The major aim of this study was to explore the relationship between social responsibility and preference for immediate, smaller rewards as opposed to delayed, larger rewards. It was hypothesized that subjects preferring immediate rewards would show less social responsibility than subjects preferring larger delayed rewards.

Trinidad Negro children, 12 to 14 years old, were tested. One hundred thirty-six were from a large elementary government school and 70 from a boys' industrial school for juvenile delinquents. An instrument was administered to measure social responsibility.

The primary findings included the following:
1. delinquents showed greater preference for immediate smaller reinforcement;
2. subjects who preferred immediate, smaller rewards tended to have lower social responsibility scores;
3. accuracy in recalling the time of a past event was related to preference for delayed reinforcement.

C,F,A

Montague, D. O., 1964.
Arithmetic concepts of kindergarten children in contrasting socioeconomic areas.
Elem. sch. J., 64, 393-397.

An investigation of social-class differences in arithmetic concepts in kindergarten children was conducted.

The Arithmetic Concepts Inventory constructed by A. K. Ruddell was administered to 51 low socioeconomic status (SES) and 31 high socio-economic status kindergarten children who had been in school for seven months. The inventory includes subtests of Enumeration, Quantitative Relationships, Symbol Recognition, Social Usage, and Problem Solving.

A significant difference between classes on total score on the inventory was found. The lower SES pupils were lower on the arithmetic concepts tests.

150

Mussen, P., 1953.
Differences between the TAT responses of Negro and white boys.
J. consult. Psychol., 17, 373-376.

This study investigated differences between the content of TAT stories of Negro and white children in New York City.

Thirteen TAT cards were administered to lower-class Negro and white boys who were vacationing at the summer camp of a social agency. Fifty Negro and 50 white boys of normal intelligence were matched so that equal numbers were assigned to each age level between 9 and 14. Twenty-eight needs and 22 press categories were employed in analysis of the protocols. TAT scores above the mean for the total group were considered high, those below the mean were considered low.

Analysis of 50 chi-squares yielded 14 values significant at the .05 level or better. "The Negro subject's stories contained significantly more incidents of aggressive press from the environment and mild, verbal aggressive expression by heroes. Compared with the whites, they showed less interest in establishing and maintaining friendly relations, or being kind to, or respecting others. The Negro boy's attitudes of indifference were further shown in their infrequent use of need Achievement and their emphasis on essentially inactive pursuits such as thinking and speculating. The white boys seem to suffer more from feelings of rejection in the family and more frequently express extreme hostility in their fantasies. On the other hand, they see others as respecting them and following their leadership and they respond to the generally favorable social situation by establishing friendly relations, being considerate of others, and striving to achieve something creditable."

Neugarten, Bernice L., 1946.
Social class and friendships among school children.
Amer. J. Sociol., 51, 305-313.

This study examined the relationship between the
social-class position of the family and a child's
choice of friends and his reputation among other
children.

Sociometric opinion polls and questionnaires were
administered to 174 fifth- and sixth-graders and to
206 tenth- and eleventh-graders. All the social
classes in the town were included.

A relationship was found between the socio-economic position of the family and the child's sociometric status at elementary- and at high-school levels,
both in regard to friendship and reputation. Higher-
class children were more popular as friends and had
better reputations. Both age groups made distinctions along class lines in picking friends. The
choices of the older children regarding children not
wanted for friends did not show social-class distinctions.

Osborne, R. T., 1960.
Racial differences in mental growth and school a-
chievement; a longitudinal study.
Psychol. Rep., 7, 233-239.

The California Achievement and Mental Maturity
Tests were administered to 815 white and 446 Negro
children in a southeastern state longitudinally
through grades 6, 8, and 10. Differences in reading
and arithmetic achievement between the two groups
increased from grade 6 to grade 10, with Negro group
lower.

Difference on reading scores (vocabulary and comprehension) increased from about 2 grades in grade 6
to more than 3 grades in grade 10. Arithmetic reasoning showed a 1-grade difference at grades 6 and 8
and about a 3-grade difference at grade 10. Performance on arithmetic fundamentals showed a difference of 1 grade at grade 6, about 2 grades at grade

8, and 4 grades at grade 10. In all cases the white
group was at or close to the expected national grade
norm.

Mental age showed a 2-year difference at grade 6
and almost a 4-grade difference at grade 10. "For
the Negro group achievement and mental maturity
growth became negatively accelerated or leveled off
in the 14 to 16 age range. At the latest testing
regression effect tended to reduce the range and
variability of M.A. scores."

A,D

Pasamanick, B. and Knobloch, Hilda, 1958.
Contribution of some organic factors to school re-
tardation in Negro children.
J. Negro. Educ., 27, 4-9.

This is a discussion of prenatal influences on
development based on studies of Negro and white subjects from varying social strata. "Cerebral palsy,
mental deficiency, epilepsy, childhood behavior disorders, and reading disability have been found to be
associated with complications of pregnancy, chiefly
hypertension and bleeding and prematurity." Complications of pregnancy and prematurity are associated
with lower socio-economic status and are also more
common among Negroes. Nutritional factors may be
causative. Authors suggest that Ausubel's finding
that girls have less behavior disorders, reading dis-
abilities, and more adequate adjustment may be explained in part by a relatively higher frequency of
birth complications and prematurity for males.

D,A,E

Pettigrew, T., 1964.
Negro American intelligence: a new look at an old
controversy.
J. Negro. Educ., 33, 6-25.

This is a summary of the relevant research on
Negro-white intelligence, with particular attention
to the more recent research. He presents the "Scientific racist position" of one group of workers,
but devotes the major portion of the article to the
"modern psychological position" which favors a non-

genetic interpretation of the typically lower intelligence score averages of Negro groups. The relevant research is discussed in terms of new theoretical conceptions, factors affecting intellectual underdevelopment, varying opportunities, and the individual versus the group. It is concluded from the array of research presented that the overwhelming opinion of modern psychologists supports the notion that the mean differences observed between Negro and white children are largely the result of environmental rather than genetic factors, and that intelligence is a plastic product of inherited structure developed by environmental stimulation and opportunity.

The severely deprived environment of the average Negro child can lower his measured IQ in two ways:
1. it can act to deter his actual intellectual development by presenting him with such a constricted encounter with the world that his innate potential is barely tapped, and
2. it can act to mask his actual functioning intelligence in the test situation by not preparing him culturally and motivationally for such a middle-class task.

D,C

Piaget, J., and Inhelder, Barbel, 1947.
Diagnosis of mental operations and theory of intelligence.
Amer. J. ment. Defic., 51, 401-406.

Two criticisms were made of metric scales of intelligence as being insufficient methods of diagnosis of the abnormal child's mental functioning: (1) "A test only gives us results on efficiency of mental activity without grasping the psychological operations in themselves...the test provides the sum of successes and failures, which is the actual result of past activities and attainments, but it leaves untouched the way in which these have been reached. (2) Mental age, in reference to a scale of average efficiency, does not correspond to any natural phase of mental development....the fact that a child succeeds in any one test does not necessarily imply that he will have succeeded in all those of lower age-groups....Such a method falls short of grasping the

154

advance of mental activity with age, the latter being characterized by an integration of lower levels
into the superior ones."

In light of these criticisms, the authors suggest
that a series of tests should be made up in order
that success in B test would presuppose success in A
test, etc., (a Guttman scale), which could be attained by qualitative and genetic analysis of the
operations involved in any psychological action.
Such scales are illustrated with the development of
notions of conservation of matter, weight and volume, which follow each other in succession necessarily by logical implication for all children, thus
making it possible to place abnormal phenomena of
feeble-minded reasoning at a stage of mental evolu-
tion.

D,F,C

Raab, S., Deutsch, M., and Freedman, A. M., 1960.
Perceptual shifting and set in normal school children
of different reading achievement levels.
Percept. mot. Skills, 10, 187-192.

A pilot study to investigate the relationship between reading achievement and ability to shift response from one sensory modality to another used 24
children in fourth and fifth grade in New York City.
Fourteen good readers and ten poor readers were compared on a reaction-time task that used light and
sound stimuli.

"Poor readers showed significantly greater difficulty in making a cross-modal shift than normal readers; both good and poor readers formed sets to light
but formed no sets to sound." Although the groups
differed in IQ, the performance on the reaction-time
task showed no significant relationship to IQ and the
authors suggest that modality shifting may be tapping
the "relationship between perception and reading."

D,C

Rapier, Jacqueline, L. 1962.
Measured intelligence and the ability to learn.
Acta Psychol., 20 (1), 1-17.

The author reviewed some of the literature which
challenged the belief in the inherent relation between intelligence and learning. Woodrow in an
earlier review had argued that test users who identified intelligence with learning had confused a-
chievement with the ability to gain with practice
and that individuals do not possess a unitary general
learning ability. Measures of learning in the laboratory and in the school, however, did not support
such a belief, but the experimental evidence was open
to criticism for weaknesses in methodology. Improvement of methodology was difficult, particularly in
terms of finding reliable and representative learning measures.

More recent research is reviewed which offers
fresh approaches to the problem. Some investigators
have used subnormals as subjects and have shown that
they can compete with normals in certain learning
situations. Other investigators explain the often-
reported lack of relationship between intelligence
and learning as an effect of individual differences
in learning and have turned to an investigation of
the learning process itself to observe what happens
at different stages of learning. Another approach is
represented by investigators who are concerned with
broadening knowledge of intelligence by discovering
more of the factors that make up intellectual ability.

E,A

Reis, A. J. and Rhodes, A. L., 1959.
Are educational norms and goals of conforming, truant
and delinquent adolescents influenced by group position in American society?
J. Negro Educ., 28 (3), 252-267.

This paper described the educational achievement
goals and the value placed on schooling by an adolescent population. Questionnaires were used to gather
information from pupils in Grades 7-12 in public,

private, and parochial schools of Nashville, Tennessee. (N approximately 22,000)

Each of the following vary substantially with race, sex, IQ, and socio-economic status:
1. Perception of how much education most people ought to get
2. Adolescents' evaluation of how important schooling is to them
3. How far their mothers expect them to go in school
4. How far they want to go in school
5. Their desire to quit school
6. To quit school because one is forced to go
7. To quit school and go to work

Delinquents and truants are more likely to want to quit school and get a job than they are to want to quit school because they regard compulsory school attendance as coercive. Negro adolescents value schooling more than white adolescents and are more achievement oriented in terms of their educational aspirations. The age, sex, IQ, and SES of the Negro is of less influence on his behavior than his race position as compared to white adolescents.

A,E,D,G

Riessman, F., 1962.
The culturally deprived child.
New York: Harper.

This book draws on personal experience and empirical literature in an attempt to adequately characterize the culturally deprived child and to suggest action implications for the school. Among the major conclusions are the following:

1. The culturally deprived desire education more than is generally recognized, but the reasons for wanting education are not those stressed by the school. The school emphasizes education for its own sake and to develop self-expression, whereas the culturally deprived are usually interested in education for vocational reasons, to get along in the modern world, or because of a high respect for science.

157

2. Strengths and weaknesses of the culturally deprived can be tentatively listed. <u>Weaknesses</u>:
   "narrowness of traditionalism, pragmatism,
   anti-intellectualism; limited development of
   individualism and creativity; alienation;
   political apathy; suggestibility and naivete;
   boring occupation tasks; crowded homes."
   <u>Strengths</u>: "cooperativeness and mutual aid of
   extended families; lack of strain accompany-
   ing competition and individualism; equalitari-
   anism, informality and humor; freedom from
   self-blame and parental overprotection;
   lessened sibling rivalry, security found in
   the extended family and in a traditional outlook."
3. Characteristics of deprived child's style:
   (a) "physical and visual rather than aural,
   (b) content-centered rather than form-cen-
   tered, (c) externally oriented rather than
   introspective, (d) problem-centered rather
   than abstract-centered, (e) inductive rather
   than deductive, (f) spatial rather than temporal, (g) slow, careful, persevering (in
   areas of importance), rather than quick, fa-
   cile, flexible, (h) definite lack of formal
   language skills, but high development of informal language and gestures."

E,A

Rosen, B. C., 1956.
The achievement syndrome: a psychocultural dimen-
sion of social stratification.
Amer. Sociol. Rev., 21, 203-211.

This study examined the notion that social classes
in America are characterized by a dissimilar concern
with achievement, particularly as expressed in the
striving for status through social mobility. It was
hypothesized that social classes differ in possession
of two components of achievement orientation: (1) a
personality characteristic called achievement motivation, and (2) value orientations which define and
implement achievement-motivated behavior.

One hundred twenty male, white high school students, 14 to 16 years old, from differing social

classes in the New Haven area were given a Thematic Apperception Test which was scored for achievement motivation and a questionnaire, part of which contained items to measure value orientation. Questionnaire responses which were future-oriented, activistic, and individualistic in point of view were considered to reflect values most likely to facilitate achievement and social mobility.

Middle-class boys were found to have higher achievement-motivation scores than lower-class boys. Similarly, the middle-class boys had achievement-oriented values. Generally, high motivation scores were related to high grades in school, but value orientations were not. Educational aspiration was related to value orientation but not to motivation scores.

The author suggested that achievement value orientations are conceptual and probably acquired through fairly complex verbal communication, while achievement motivation probably originates earlier in parent-child interaction and is likely to be emotional and unverbalized. Thus, the achievement value and the achievement motive can be independent, though they often occur together. It seems that middle-class children are more likely to be taught both the motivation and the values that make achievement possible.

A,E

Rosen, B. C. and D'Andrade, R., 1959.
The psycho-social origins of achievement motivation.
Sociometry, 22, 185-218.

This study examined the origins of achievement motivation (need achievement) within the context of the individual's membership in family and social class.

Forty white boys about ten years of age, matched on IQ by group, were studied. Twenty were high on need achievement and 20 low as measured by TAT procedures; ten in each group were middle class and ten were lower class. Each boy in the presence of his father and mother was given a number of experimental

tasks which gave the parents opportunity to interact
with the child.

From the observations in these experimental situations, it was concluded that:
1. Fathers and mothers provide achievement training and independence training, but fathers
   contribute more to independence training of
   boys than mothers do.
2. Mothers of boys with high achievement motivation stress achievement training and they are
   more dominant and expect less self-reliance
   than mothers of boys with low achievement
   motivation. The mothers of boys with higher
   achievement motivation reward their sons with
   approval and punish them with hostility.
3. For high achievement to develop the boy appears to need more autonomy from his father
   than from his mother.
4. No difference is found by social class. However, it is believed that the matching of boys
   on need achievement and the other variables
   cancels out differences in training practices
   which might normally differentiate the social
   classes.

G,F,D,E

Schreiber, D., 1958.
Identifying and developing able students from less
privileged groups.
High Points, 40, 5-23.

This article is an early report on the Pilot Demonstration Guidance Project, later known as the
Higher Horizons program, conducted at New York City's
Manhattanville Junior High School. The program,
which began in 1956, had as its purpose the early
identification and stimulation of able students, especially students from low status socio-economic and
culturally deprived homes, to continue their education through college.

Students were selected on the basis of their cumu-
lative record, SRA Non-Verbal Intelligence Test,
Stanford-Reading Test, Stanford-Arithmetic Test,
Draw-A-Person Test scores, plus their sixth- and

eighth-grade scores on standardized tests of intelligence, reading, and arithmetic, and the evaluation of the teacher of their major subject. Ten criteria in all were used to identify the able children. Students who scored 4 or more in the criteria were selected for the experimental group which comprised 50 per cent of the student body. A total of 717 students participated in the special programs.

The program included remedial reading, mathematics, and speech, group and individual guidance with stress on college and career-planning, and cultural enrichment. The project also tried to improve the self-images of the participating students and to develop pride in their cultural background (40 per cent of the student body were Puerto Rican and 45 per cent were Negroes). Parent education and participation in school activities were also encouraged. A Scholarship Fund made it possible for students unable to pay to participate in some of the special events.

Some of the results reported for the Pilot Demonstration Guidance Project follow:
1. Median gain for the first 7 months in remedial reading was 1.4 years; individual gains were as high as 5.4 years;
2. Median gain in remedial mathematics was 1.2 years; individual gains were as high as 4.5 years;
3. Median score on the Stanford Reading Test given the ninth-grade experimental group showed a gain of 15.8 months in paragraph meaning; 172 eighth-graders showed a gain of 2 years in comprehension, 2.2 years in vocabulary, and 2.1 years for the total Stanford Reading Test over a period of 1.4 years that had elapsed between tests.

It was concluded that supposedly uneducable children from lower socio-economic backgrounds can successfully learn and progress in a reorganized school environment. The parents as well as the children were enthusiastic about the program.

Sears, Pauline S., 1940.
Levels of aspiration in academically successful and
unsuccessful children.
J. abnorm. soc. Psychol., 35, 498-536.

The hypothesis of this study was that one factor
in the level of aspiration pattern for a given task
is the characteristic past experience of success or
failure which the individual associates with that
task.

Past experience of success or failure was evaluated on the basis of achievement in the academic
school subjects of reading and arithmetic in children
in grades 4, 5, and 6. Tasks used to determine level
of aspiration were derived from reading (multiple-
choice word-meaning items) and arithmetic (problems
in addition). A "success" (success in both reading
and arithmetic), a "failure" (low in reading and
arithmetic), and a "differential" group (prior success with reading, failure with arithmetic) were designated. These three groups matched on age (mental
and chronological) and sex had 12 subjects each. The
tasks were administered to the sample as speed tests.
The subject was first told his performance time and
was subsequently asked for his level of aspiration on
the next task. A series of 20 tasks were presented
to each subject. A discrepancy score was calculated;
this score was the difference between the actual performance time and the stated level of aspiration.

The "failure" group when compared with the "success" group showed larger discrepancy scores and
greater variability in discrepancy scores. The
"differential" group showed lower discrepancy scores
on reading but larger values on arithmetic; these results resembled those of the "success" group on reading and those of the "failure" group on arithmetic.
Differences between the "differential" and the "success" groups in reading and between the "differential" and "failure" groups in arithmetic were small.
The results are consistent with the hypothesis that
attitudes of success and failure influence levels of
aspiration.

C,D

Semler, I. J. and Iscoe, I., 1963.
Comparative and developmental study of the learning
abilities of Negro and white children under four
conditions.
J. educ. Psychol., 54, 38-44.

Object pairs and picture pairs of the same objects in conceptually similar and dissimilar sets
provided 4 experimental conditions for comparing
paired-associate learning of 135 Negro subjects with
141 white subjects across age levels 5 to 9 years.

Full-scale WISC IQs were found to be significantly
lower for Negro than for white subjects (<.001)
across all ages but differences in paired-associate
learning favoring white subjects at lower age levels
disappeared by 9 years of age.

Racial differences were greatest on IQ at the 5-
year level, probably because of the particular lower
socio-economic status nursery center from which the
subjects were drawn; however, negligible correlations
were obtained between learning-task scores and IQ for
both races (.094 for whites and .189 for Negroes).
Associating object pairs in conceptually similar sets
was easiest and picture pairs in dissimilar sets most
difficult for both races.

The authors conclude that "Our findings of no
overall race differences in learning ability should
not be minimized. They suggest that educators should
exercise greatest caution in inferring learning ability from measured intellectual levels alone."

E,A

Sewell, W. H., Haller, A. O., and Straus, M. A., 1957.
Social status and educational and occupational aspir-
ation.
Amer. Sociol. Rev., 22, 67-73.

This study tested the general hypothesis that
levels of educational and occupational aspiration of
young people of both sexes are associated with the
social status of their families, when the effects of
intelligence are controlled.

Questionnaires were administered to a random sample of all non-farm seniors in public and private high schools in Wisconsin; sample size was 4,167. Data for educational aspiration were taken from responses to a series of questions concerning education the student planned to obtain after graduation. Data on the level of occupational aspiration were taken from a question concerning the vocation the student planned to enter. Social status was measured by the prestige of parental occupation; data were taken from a question on the present occupation of the student's parent. Students were arranged into five equal-sized, rank-ordered categories on the basis of parental prestige and on the basis of intelligence.

The findings support the idea that values associated with status position are important influences on educational and occupational aspirations. For both males and females, when intelligence is controlled, there is a significant positive relationship between level of educational aspiration and parental social status. Similarly, there is a positive relation between level of occupational aspiration and parental social status.

G

Shaw, F., 1963.
Educating culturally deprived youth in urban centers.
Phi Delta Kappan, 45, 91-97.

The purpose of this article was to examine the problem of educating culturally disadvantaged children and to describe how some of the nation's larger school systems are dealing with the problem. Specific examples were cited from the 1959 Detroit project and the 1959 New York Higher Horizons Project.

The following were seen as common features of both the projects:
1. Classroom teachers' work is reinforced by professional workers and by smaller classes;
2. The schools work to show the parents that education can open new opportunities for the children;
3. The entire community is involved;
4. Additional funds are provided.

164

Some other features of these programs are Special
Service Schools to offer the students extra help;
early identification and, hopefully, prevention of
deprivation; programs for non-English speaking children; and career guidance programs.

The major conclusion seems to be that researchers
are beginning to see hopeful signs in the education
of the culturally deprived.

C,D,F,A

Siller, J., 1957.
Socio-economic status and conceptual thinking.
J. abnorm. soc. Psychol., 55, 365-371.

This study tests the following hypotheses:
1. High-status (HS) children score higher than
    low-status (LS) children on all tests of con-
    ceptual ability.
2. Form of symbolism contributes to status diff-
    erences--greater difference predicted on ver-
    bal than on non-verbal material.
3. When alternative correct answers are available
    which differ along an abstractness-concrete
    dimension, HS children will more frequently
    select abstract answers than LS children.
4. When subjects are matched on non-verbal
    scores, HS children score higher than LS on
    tests of verbal concepts dealing with the same
    kind of conceptualization as the non-verbal
    tests.
5. When subjects are matched on verbal-concept
    tests, LS children score more highly than HS
    children on tests of non-verbal concepts deal-
    ing with the same kind of conceptualization as
    the verbal tests.

Subjects were 181 white sixth-grade children (99
middle class and 82 low status). Mean IQ on Otis was
118 for HS and 103 for LS groups. Mean reading
scores on Metropolitan tests were 8.03 for HS and
5.97 for LS. Instruments used were verbal and non-
verbal classification tests, verbal and non-verbal
analogies tests, and vocabulary test with definitions
varying along concrete-abstract dimensions.

Results showed Hypotheses 1 and 2 fully confirmed. Choice of definition types showed a tendency toward abstraction which was significantly greater for HS group than for LS group, but author notes that order of preference of types of definitions is identical for both groups. Hypothesis 4 was confirmed, but Hypothesis 5 was not.

When, however, groups were matched on IQ, none of the differences described remained. The author indicates that this is due to dropping of lower extreme of the low-status group and suggests that status differences in conceptual ability which are usually noted may be largely attributable to the existence of a group of extremely low scorers in the LS group. He suggests that this very low group may come from families which are not striving for mobility, but does not have the data to investigate this question.

E,A

Silverman, Susan B., 1963.
Self-images of upper-middle class and working class young adolescents.
Unpublished masters thesis, University of Chicago.

It was hypothesized that differences between social classes in personality (self-image) should exist because of differential socialization and value orientations. Using the work of Kahl and Sears, the general prediction was made that working-class children would be characterized by repressive behavior patterns and upper middle-class children would be characterized by expressive behavior.

A form of the semantic differential was administered to 190 upper middle-class subjects (100 male, 90 female) and 134 working-class subjects (56 male, 78 female). All subjects were white and in seventh and eighth grades; average age was 13 years.

The main hypotheses regarding class differences in self-images were supported. In particular, ratings in the direction of respectability and restraint were marked in the working class and not so evident in the upper-middle class. As was predicted, class differences were more evident for the boys than for the girls.

166

Within each social class a sex-differential emerged. In the upper-middle class expressive (independent) behavior seemed particularly evident in the boys, while the girls seemed to exhibit an element of restraint. In the working class the boys seemed most "internal" or restrained and the girls showed an element of expressiveness.

It was suggested that the respectability orientation of the working class contains elements which may make progressive educational methods incompatible with the cultural orientation.

G,D,C,A

Smilansky, Sarah, 1964.
Progress report on a program to demonstrate ways of using a year of kindergarten to promote cognitive abilities, impart basic information and modify attitudes which are essential for scholastic success of culturally deprived children in their first two years of school. Henrietta Szold Institute, Jerusalem, Israel, Ditto.

This is a report of a kindergarten program designed to improve the educational readiness of low-status Oriental Jewish children. The program was aimed at working toward "school requirements, on the one hand, and on making good the children's deficiences, on the other."

Four experimental and four control kindergarten classes were studied. The program used regular teachers and normal class size of 35 children, but experimental teachers were given assistance and some materials by specialists. The objectives for the experimental kindergarten program were carefully detailed. Control groups had regular kindergarten instruction. Three hundred six five-year old children were studied.

After the kindergarten year, the experimental groups were significantly higher than the controls on the Stanford-Binet and WISC intelligence tests. An average of a six-point difference on the S-B and a ten-point difference on the WISC were reported in favor of the experimental groups. The lower the initial IQ of the child, the greater the gain over the year, but all experimental-group children showed some gain, even those starting with above average IQs.

E,A

Smith, H. P. and Anderson, Marcia, 1962.
Racial and family experience correlates of mobility aspiration.
J. Negro Educ., 31, 117-124.

Thirty-three Negro and 33 white high school students, matched for age, sex, intelligence, and social status (upper-lower and lower-lower), served as subjects to test the relationship between mobility aspiration (Rosen's achievement syndrome), race, and family experience measured by a questionnaire on affectional patterns in the family (devised by Dynes).

The results as a whole showed no consistent association between the independent variables and mobility aspiration. Negroes and whites did not differ in achievement motivation. The achievement value orientation of the whites was significantly higher than that of the Negroes (Rosen's scale). The Negroes had significantly higher educational and vocational aspirations and, in contrast to the whites, valued success more than happiness in their careers. There was no relationship between the measure of family experiences (satisfactory-unsatisfactory) and mobility aspiration.

The authors concluded that the tendency of Negro youth to have higher educational-vocational aspirations seems to be on a fantasy level rather than a reality level. The study failed to confirm relationships found by Rosen and by Clark, Dynes, and Dinitz between race, family experience, and mobility aspiration.

G, E, A

Stendler, Celia B., 1951.
Social class differences in parental attitude toward
school at grade 1 level.
Child Develpm., 22, 37-46.

Data with regard to parental belief in and support
of the school at grade 1 level were collected by
means of parent interviews and analyzed for possible
social-class differences. These data were in five
different areas: preschool attendance, parental
educational aspirations for the child, preparation
for school, parental criticism of the school, parental reception of report card.

Two interviews were completed with 212 parents
whose children were to enter first grade in the fall.
Parents were typed as to social class using the
Warner, Meeker, and Eells technique. Five social
classes were defined.

The results showed, with regard to educational
aspirations, that parental expectations for children
became less ambitious "as one goes down the social
ladder." Half of the lower-class mothers, however,
reported that they expected their children to finish
high school which contrasts sharply with per cent of
lower-class students who did finish high school at
the time this article was written. No social-class
differences were found in parental criticisms of the
school.

E, F, A

Stivers, E., 1958.
Motivation for college in high-school boys.
School Rev., 66, 341-350.

This was a study of high school students in the
upper quarter of their class in academic ability to
determine the source of motivation for college.

Forty-one boys at the tenth-grade level (31 motivated for college and 10 non-motivated for college)
were studied. A number of aptitude tests (Primary
Mental Abilities, Davis-Eells, Goodenough-Draw-A-Man
Test, etc.) were used to determine academic ability.

Warner's Index of Status Characteristics, McClelland's TAT procedure to measure need Achievement, interviews to determine predisposing experiences, and the California Psychological Inventory were also administered.

Findings:
1. Need achievement is the most important variable determining motivation for college in this sample.
2. A large number of persons representing various socializing agencies (family, peer group, school) had set college as a standard of achievement for college-motivated boys.
3. In this sample very little difference in social status was found between motivated and non-motivated boys.
4. Some differences on the California Psychological Inventory such as Independence and Autonomy favored the motivated boys.
5. On the Strodtbeck value scale the motivated boys had more values associated with academic and status-oriented achievement.
6. Motivated boys were more active in religious groups.

The author concluded that college-going is not a result of middle-class socialization in general, but more particularly of experiences with parents, teachers, peers, and others who as early as elementary school set college as a standard of achievement for the student.

E,F,A

Stivers, E., 1959.
Motivation for college in high-school girls.
School Rev., 67, 320-334.

This is part of a larger study of the sources of motivation for college in high school students in the upper fourth of ability. The author studied 45 girls in tenth grade (32 motivated for college, and 13 non-motivated for college). Aptitude tests, Index of Social Status, McClelland's TAT need achievement, interviews, and California Psychological Inventory were administered.

Findings:
1. Social class was the most important variable differentiating the two groups (different from results for boys).
2. Need achievement was slightly higher for non-motivated students than for college-motivated students (different from results for boys).
3. A large number of persons representing various socializing agencies had set college as a standard of achievement for motivated group (same as boys).
4. Motivated students had higher scores in Personal and Intellectual Efficiency on the California inventory.

It was concluded that social roles for women make it possible for able women with high need achievement to find their careers in homemaking rather than in professions requiring college.

E,C,A

Terrel, G. Jr., Durkin, Kathryn, and Wiesley, M., 1959.
Social class and the nature of the incentive in discrimination learning.
J. abnorm. soc. Psychol., 59, 270-272.

The purpose of this study was to test the hypothesis that a non-material incentive is as effective as a material incentive for middle-class pupils, while for lower-class pupils a material incentive is more effective than a non-material one.

There were 12 subjects in each of the following age categories: 5, 6, 10, and 11-year-olds, with an equal number of boys and girls in each group. Warner's Index of Status Characteristics was used to determine class position. Three-dimensional geometric figures in the shape of cubes, cones, and cylinders were used. The geometric figures within each set differed in size. Each subject was asked to make a response on a specified criterion. One group of subjects received a non-material reward, a light flash, while the subjects of the other group were asked to respond and then received a material reward, a small piece of candy in addition to the light flash. All subjects were designated as members of either the middle-class group or the lower-class group.

The authors found that middle-class children learned more quickly when given a non-material incentive than when given a material incentive, while the reverse was true of lower-class children.

B

Thomas, D., 1963.
Oral language, sentence structure and vocabulary of kindergarten children living in low socio-economic urban areas.
Unpublished doctoral dissertation, Wayne University.

This study investigated the oral language of 50 white and 50 Negro low socio-economic status kindergarten children by use of a structured interview.

Main findings:
1. Some Negro deficiency in oral language as compared to white, but much similarity. Negroes used fewer mature sentence types and made more specific grammatical errors.
2. Few sex differences found in contrast to earlier work in the field.
3. Vocabulary of these children differs quantitatively and qualitatively from that of readers and standard word lists.

Includes extensive lists of word counts and typical grammatical structure for lower socio-economic status children.

D,B,G

Weaver, S. J., 1963.
Interim report: psycholinguistic abilities of culturally deprived children.
George Peabody College for Teachers, Mimeo.

Illinois Test of Psycholinguistic Abilities was administered to 61 Negro subjects in Early Training Project for the culturally deprived child. Pattern of both experimental and control groups indicates strength in visual-motor patterns and deficit on auditory-vocal channels. Experimental groups

172

(varying amounts of summer school and home contact program) showed significantly higher scores on overall language development than the controls. In particular, visual decoding, auditory-vocal association, and visual-motor sequencing showed strong differences after training programs. Subjects entered program at approximately age 3 1/2 and were about five years old at testing. Possible sex differences are indicated (lower for boys).

Data indicates the possibility of changing psycholinguistic abilities through training.

                                                    B,G,F
Weiner, M. and Feldmann, Shirley, 1963.
Validation studies of a reading prognosis test for children of lower and middle socio-economic status. Educ. psychol. Measmt., 23, 807-814.

An individually administered reading prognosis test for use with kindergarten and first-grade children was developed and validated on 138 children including lower socio-economic status subjects. Test measures: Language (word meaning and storytelling), Perceptual Discrimination (visual similarities, visual discrimination, and auditory discrimination), and Beginning Reading Skills (capital alphabet letters, small alphabet letters, and sight vocabulary).

Test validated at year end on Gates Primary Reading Tests (Sentence reading and Paragraphs). Prediction for entire group showed r = .81 for Paragraph test and r = .78 for Sentence test. All subtests correlated .52 and higher with criteria except Storytelling (.23 with Sentences and .29 with Paragraphs) and Auditory Discrimination (.18 with Sentences and .19 with Paragraphs). Authors conclude that skill deficiencies underlying reading can be measured in children from any socio-economic group before reading instruction begins.

Weiner, M. and Murray, W., 1963.
Another look at the culturally deprived and their
levels of aspiration.
J. educ. Sociol., '36, 319-321.

The authors attempted to account for conflicting
evidence regarding aspiration levels of parents from
different social levels. It was suggested that parents at different levels may have the same level of
aspiration for their children, but that the upper-
status groups are more certain that their aspirations may be fulfilled.

In a study in Westchester County it was found
that most parents and children at lower and upper
levels listed professional occupations as goals.
However, only 37 per cent of the lower-status children were taking the college preparatory course
while 100 per cent of middle-class children were
taking college preparatory course.

The authors suggested that methods of adult education might be used to help lower-status parents
become aware of ways in which their aspirations can
be increasingly fulfilled.

Wellman, Beth L. and McCandless, B. R., 1946.
Factors associated with Binet IQ changes of pre-
school children.
Psychol. Monogr., 60, 2 (Whole No. 278).

The purpose of this study was to measure the effects of various experiences in preschool on IQ
changes and vocabulary development.

The first unit of the investigation involved 66
children ranging in age from 35 to 58 months. The
children were observed over an average interval of
5.6 months for selected types of teacher-child and
child-child contacts thought to be relevant to intelligence. Teacher-child categories were: chan-
nelizes activity, gives physical help, gives information, and asks leading questions. Subjects
were tested and re-tested with the Stanford-Binet,

Form L. No relationship was found between IQ change
and frequency of teacher-child or child-child contacts of the type studied.

The Smith-Williams vocabulary test was administered in the fall and again in the spring to 34 subjects, age 38 to 61 months. Vocabulary and IQ correlated .71 for the fall measures and .75 for the
spring tests. There was no relationship between
change in vocabulary and change in IQ. Teacher contacts showed a correlation of +.47 with vocabulary
change for 18 children who were new to the preschool.

Children whose vocabulary sigma score in the fall
was higher than their M.A. sigma score gained significantly in IQ (7.6 points) during the year, while
those whose vocabulary standing was lower than their
M.A. standing did now show appreciable gain (.6 IQ
points). Subjects who increased their superiority
of vocabulary over M.A. tended to receive more teacher contacts than those who moved in the opposite
direction; the contacts appearing to be more effective for new entrants than for children previously
enrolled. It should be noted that the mean fall IQ
of these children was 120.5, the mean spring IQ
124.9, the mean change in IQ 4.4 points, with 33 per
cent of the group gaining 10 or more points.

D,B,F

Wepman, J. M., 1960.
Auditory discrimination, speech, and reading.
Elem. School J., 60, 325-333.

Auditory discrimination and its relationship to
speech and reading were investigated. The main hypothesis is that auditory discrimination is attained
gradually and often as late as the age of 8.

The author distinguishes three levels of audition
which develop sequentially.
1. Acuity is the ability of the ear to collect
   sounds and transmit them to the nervous system.

2. Understanding is the ability to extract and interpret meaning from sound patterns.
3. Discrimination and retention are the abilities which permit the individual to differentiate each sound from every other sound and to hold each sound in mind well enough and long enough to make accurate phonic comparisons.

Wepman Auditory Discrimination Test was administered to 80 first-graders and 76 second-graders. There was a decreasing number of children with poor auditory discrimination--26 per cent in grade 1 and 19 per cent in grade 2. Children with poor discrimination tended to be poorer readers, but the major effect of poor discrimination was reflected in poor speech articulation.

The author concluded that since auditory discrimination often develops more fully in the first years of school, speech therapy should not be initiated in children who have poor discrimination (which accounts for about 80 per cent of articulation problems) until around the age of 8. He also suggested that reading instruction can be made consonant with the discrimination abilities of the children. Many first-graders would not benefit from phonic reading instruction and these children are identifiable.

E,F,G

Wilson, A. B., 1959.
Residential segregation of social classes and aspirations of high school boys.
Amer. Sociol. Rev., 24, 836-845.

This was an investigation of the role of the school climate and group membership in shaping aspirations for education and academic achievement in high school boys. Eight different high schools in the San Francisco-Oakland area were studied. Schools varied in proportion of students coming from different status levels.

It was found that in predominantly lower-status schools, the proportion of middle-class boys who planned to go to college was significantly lower than in predominantly middle-class schools. A lower-class boy was more likely to plan to attend college if he was enrolled in a predominantly middle-class school than if he was enrolled in a lower-status school. Academic achievement was affected in a similar way.

The author concluded that residential segregation of social classes in cities results in schools with unequal climates which affect the motivation of the child by providing a different ethos in which to perceive values.

D,A

Wolf, R. M., 1964.
The identification and measurement of environmental process variables related to intelligence.
Unpublished doctoral dissertation, University of Chicago.

The author hypothesized that 13 process variables could be used to describe the interactions between parents and children insofar as intelligence development is concerned. These process variables were classified under: Press for Achievement Motivation, Press for Language Development, and Provision for General Learning. He devised an interview form and interviewed the mothers of 60 fifth-grade students in a midwestern community. He then rated each family or home on each of the 13 process variables. He found a multiple correlation of +.76 between these ratings and Henmon-Nelson IQ. This correlation may be contrasted with the correlations of +.40 or less between intelligence and such environmental variables as social status, parent's occupation, or parent's education.

This method of measuring environmental process variables may be used to analyze the ways in which an environment can have a relatively direct influence on general intelligence and it should provide a method of measuring the environment for various kinds of experimental research on the problems involved in the development of intelligence.

E,F,D

Wylie, Ruth C., 1963.
Children's estimates of their schoolwork ability, as
a function of sex, race, and socio-economic status.
J. Personal., 31, 203-224.

Three kinds of estimates of their ability to do
schoolwork were made by 823 junior high school children. IQs were used as a rough external criterion
of this kind of ability. The results supported the
following hypotheses which were based on the assumed
importance of cultural learning in the development
of self-evaluations of ability: (1) white girls
make more modest estimates of their ability than do
white boys; (2) Negro subjects make more modest estimates of their ability than do white subjects; (3)
children of lower socio-economic levels make more
modest estimates of their ability than do children of
higher socio-economic levels.

In line with previous studies and with the assumption that the mechanism of denial is widely used,
the present results also show a highly significant
self-favorability bias in the group as a whole.

(Author's Summary)

C,E

Zigler, E. and DeLabry, J., 1962.
Concept switching in middle-class, lower-class and
retarded children.
J. abnorm. soc. Psychol., 65, 267-273.

This study was designed to test performance on a
concept-switching task under different reward conditions. Middle-class, lower-class and retarded
groups were matched on mental age. Intangible and
tangible rewards were used with each type of subject. The procedure yielded six experimental groups,
with eleven subjects in each group.

It was hypothesized that the middle-class subjects
would perform effectively under the intangible rather
than tangible-reward condition and that the lower-
class and retarded subjects would perform more effectively under tangible reinforcement. It was

further hypothesized that the middle-class group would perform better than the other two groups under intangible reinforcement, but that no differences would be found if the optimal reinforcement was used with each group.

In general, the findings of the study supported the hypotheses. Under the intangible-reinforcement condition, the middle-class children's performance was superior to that of the other two groups. However, when the middle-class intangible group was compared with the retarded and the lower-class children under tangible reinforcement (defined as optimal reinforcement for each group), no differences in performance were found.